SO-AAC-470

a slice of organic life

EDITOR-IN-CHIEF
SHEHERAZADE GOLDSMITH

LONDON, NEW YORK,
MUNICH, MELBOURNE, DELHI

Project Editor Susannah Steel
Editor Zia Allaway
Project Designer Claire Legemah
American Editors Shannon Beatty,
Jenny Siklos

Photography Peter Anderson

Main Contributor Anne Gatti
Contributors Daphne Lambert,
Erica Bower, Pat Thomas,
Matilda Lee, Rob Yarham

Managing Editor Anna Kruger
Managing Art Editor Alison Donovan
DTP Designer Louise Waller
Picture Research Lucy Claxton,
Mel Watson
Production Controller Rebecca Short

First American edition 2007
First paperback edition 2010

Published in the United States by
DK Publishing, 375 Hudson Street,
New York, NY 10014

10 11 12 10 9 8 7 6 5 4 3 2 1

AD328 May 2010

Copyright
© 2007, 2010 Dorling Kindersley Limited
Foreword copyright © 2007, 2010 Alice Waters
Introduction © 2007, 2010 Sheherazade
Goldsmith

Without limiting the rights under copyright reserved
above, no part of this publication may be reproduced,
stored in or introduced into a retrieval system, or
transmitted, in any form, or by any means (electronic,
mechanical, photocopying, recording, or otherwise),
without the prior written permission of both the
copyright owner and the above publisher of this book.

A catalog record for this book is
available from the Library of Congress

ISBN 978-0-7566-6211-0

DK books are available at special discounts when
purchased in bulk for sales promotions, premiums,
fund-raising, or educational use. For details, contact:
DK Publishing Special Markets, 375 Hudson Street,
New York, New York 10014 or SpecialSales@dk.com.

Reproduction by Wyndehams-Icon, London
Printed and bound by
Sheck Wah Tong, China

Discover more at
www.dk.com

CONTENTS

1 NO NEED FOR A YARD

2 ROOF TERRACE, PATIO, OR TINY YARD

3 YARD, COMMUNITY GARDEN, OR FIELD

FOREWORD by Alice Waters

This beautifully illustrated book is a treasury of practical information. The projects that Sheherazade Goldsmith proposes are simple object lessons in ecology and conservation that not so long ago were part of our everyday education. We used to eat food in season, gather it locally, and eat it with family. We used to treasure varieties of fruits and vegetables for flavor. We saved paper, cleaned with vinegar and, when I was a child, we used real glass milk bottles that we returned to the milkman to be refilled at the dairy. But with the ever-increasing premiums placed on convenience and homogeneity, all this has changed. Now, with the survival of the planet at stake, we need to relearn these basic lessons in sustainability.

Like Sheherazade, I am a firm believer in the real power—the world-changing power—of small things. After all, my restaurant started in a small way. We were young and unbelievably naïve. We began our search for local farmers because we wanted to serve the freshest, best-tasting foods. Neighbors brought us bunches of radishes, sorrel, and herbs from their backyards. We found local ranchers with beautiful spring lambs and farmers who could grow perfect lettuces for us. Bit by bit, we built a network of suppliers. In the beginning, we could never have foreseen the cumulative results of our small decisions to buy from this or that local producer. But over the last three decades we've seen the impact that our choices have made: we've built a real community—one in which our growers depend upon us as much as we do on them—and one that, I think it's no exaggeration to say, has been instrumental in changing the way we eat in this country. And this is the central tenet of *A Slice of Organic Life*: that the small decisions we make can truly change the world.

INTRODUCTION by Sheherazade Goldsmith

Until a few years ago, individuals who were concerned about the state of the environment were considered alarmist. The only people really involved in any kinds of campaigns were environmentalists, who have long appeared to non-environmentalists as slightly eccentric. How could something as rich and vast as the planet be affected by our lifestyles? The possibility that we might actually be exhausting its resources was inconceivable then.

Now that is changing, and fast. You can't open a newspaper without being made aware of the impact of our lives on the planet... the extinction of species, melting glaciers, freak weather events, water shortages and so on, each more

horrifying than the next. We now know from endless scientific studies that we are actively destroying the only planet we know that can sustain us. Indeed, if everyone lived the life of the average person in the US, we would need six planets of identical natural resources in order to sustain us.

I soon began to question my own way of life and find alternatives

Until I became a mother, I was as relaxed as the next person about the state of the natural world. I was aware of the issues, but I rarely lost sleep over them, and if something grabbed my attention, I was usually able to push it to one side believing there was no point worrying—and that, in any case, the world is full of professional people devoted to tackling these trends. But worrying is what mothers do best, and with three small children of my own, stories about rising sea levels, the use of pesticides on our foods, and the increase of childhood cancers were no longer so abstract. I soon began to question my own way of life and became aware of the need to find alternatives to my existing habits.

The Iroquois people of North America demanded of their elders that they make decisions only after considering the impact it would have on the seventh generation yet to come. It seems to me that this is exactly the approach we badly need. Without it, the kind of world we might end up passing on to our grandchildren doesn't bear thinking about.

It's now clear to most people that we need to learn how to live within nature's limits. Even if you're still not fully convinced by the science of climate change, there is, nevertheless, more than enough evidence to justify taking precautions. The risk of doing nothing is too big a price to pay. We need to

> *Working with nature rather than against it only helps to simplify and enrich our lives*

convert our knowledge into action. The good news is that there are many solutions, and contrary to what we have often been led to believe, they don't involve us living deprived and boring lives where our greatest pleasures are forbidden. They are simple, affordable, and effortless.

We can do an enormous amount simply by changing our daily habits. There was a time when recycling presented itself as a chore. Today it's second nature to a growing majority of us. Choosing to buy energy-efficient light bulbs, for example, would lead to dramatic energy savings if we all did it. And if we all choose, wherever possible and within our means, to buy local food that is fresher and healthier for us, we'll be contributing to a reversing decline in our rural communities and helping to reduce emissions resulting from so-called "food miles." None of these changes represents a sacrifice.

More importantly, if we shift our lifestyles so that we're living more naturally, a whole world becomes available to us. Nature is generous,

clever, and beautiful, which is why being in contact with it, whether it be at a food market, in our gardens, or planting up a window box brings us great pleasure. Working with nature rather than against it only helps to simplify and enrich our lives.

I hope that what this book will show is that the joys of eating seasonally, growing your own food, keeping bees, making compost, or keeping chickens are real, that being more conscientious isn't about giving up things. On the contrary, it's about rediscovering the simple pleasures of life. Each of the chapters provides simple ideas and examples of how we can lessen our impact on the world and improve the quality of our lives. Some of the topics may seem insignificant, but it's impossible to exaggerate the value of acting together. We all need to eat, for instance, and so the tiniest change in the way we eat will have profound and wide-ranging implications.

It's impossible to exaggerate the value of acting together

Each one of us has a role to play in reversing the decline of our planet, whether it's turning our televisions off at the wall or installing a wood-burning stove. I'm certain that knowing you're part of the solution and not the problem is good for the soul. And with every passing day, our chances of reversing the damage to the planet increases as the number of people willing to take a stand grows. It's finally possible to be optimistic.

S. Goldsmith

1 NO NEED FOR A YARD

GROW SALAD LEAVES IN A WINDOW BOX

Baby leaf salads are a gourmet treat when eaten on their own or mixed in with a plain green salad. If you grow your own supply of succulent leaves, you can snip off a handful whenever you want to. All you need is a window box, some packets of seeds, and potting soil.

Choose a bright window ledge or shelf space for a window box, or brackets to sit a window box on. The best kind of leaves to grow are cut-and-come-again varieties. These are salads that you eat when the plants are only 2–4 in (5–10 cm) high, and which will re-sprout so that you can cut them again a few weeks later. You can get up to four cuts from one planting, depending on the kinds you grow. Not only are these baby leaves really nutritious, they taste sweeter and more succulent than many other types, and are ready to be harvested as early as three weeks after sowing. Because the leaves are picked when the plant is young, they can be grown really close together, so you will get an impressive quantity of leaves, even from a small window box.

Prepare your window box

The larger and longer the box, the less likely it is to dry out. To give the plants the best chance to grow, it should be at least 8 in (20 cm) wide and 6 in (15 cm) deep, and should have several drainage holes. It needs to be positioned in a sunny or lightly shaded spot. A plastic box is lighter and easier to move, but if you use a wooden or clay box, make sure the ledge is sturdy enough to take the weight of it when full. Sitting the box on a drainage tray helps to keep moisture in and prevents water from splashing down the wall or over the ledge.

How to grow salad leaves

Salad leaves need rich, moist, well-drained soil. Put a layer of terracotta or pebbles in the base of the window box and fill it with good-quality potting soil. Moisten the soil and sow seeds thinly from early spring onward, covering them lightly with compost. Once they have germinated, thin the seedlings. If you go away, ask a friend to water, or use a self-watering system, such as an upturned plastic bottle with the bottom cut off and small holes drilled close to the cap—fill the bottle and the water will slowly drip through the holes. Stick copper tape around the box to keep slugs and snails out. When they are finger height, cut the leaves about 1¼ in (3 cm) above the soil and leave to regrow.

For salad mixes, thin seedlings to 1¼ in (3 cm) apart.

For rocket, thin seedlings to around 6 in (15 cm) apart.

For loose-leaf lettuces Sow seeds in pots indoors in early spring, then transfer the seedlings to the window box, spacing them about 8 in (20 cm) apart.

Salad mixes

If you like a variety of flavors, try one of the salad mixes offered by seed companies. These are normally selected to blend well together—for example, spicy or Asian leaves such as mizuna, French, and Italian—and to be ready for cutting at about the same time. Some include soft-leaved herbs such as chervil and basil. Salad rocket, with a delicious peppery taste, grows particularly fast and can bolt (race to the flowering stage) in hot weather. If you have room for another window box or pot, it's worth growing salad rocket on its own. Try sowing it a bit later on for picking in the fall and winter when your other salad has stopped growing. You could also grow loose-leaf lettuces, such as "Salad bowl", "Lollo rossa", and "Catalogna" types, which you can harvest when the plants are 4–6 in (10–15 cm) high. In a 24 in (60 cm) window box, you could raise three plants, and if you choose three different varieties, you should get enough leaves to make delicious mixed salads throughout the summer.

Winter salads

You can even grow a crop of salad leaves in the winter by starting them off indoors in modules and hardening them off before planting out into the window box. In frosty weather, the crop will need to be protected with a cloche or cold frame. Good choices to try are winter purslane, mizuna, salad rocket, and corn salad.

Choose your salad leaves

Homegrown leaves taste fresher and sweeter than prepacked portions. They will grow all year, although winter growth is slower.

Summer varieties

Loose-leaf lettuce types (*Latuca sativa*) such as:

- "Salad Bowl"
- "Lollo Rossa"
- "Catalogna"
- "Bijou"
- "Bionda a Foglia 'Riccia'"
- "Oak Leaf"
- Asian mustards (*Brassica juncea*) such as "Giant Red"
- "Golden Streaks"
- Salad rocket (*Eruca sativa*)
- Mizuna (*Brassica rapa*)
- Corn salad, or "lamb's lettuce" (*Valerianella locusta*)

Winter varieties

- Winter purslane, or "claytonia" (*Montia perfoliata* or *Claytonia perfoliata*)
- Mizuna (*Brassica rapa*)
- Salad rocket (*Eruca sativa*)
- Corn salad, or "lamb's lettuce" (*Valerianella locusta*)
- Land cress, or "American cress" (*Barberea verna*)
- Asian mustard (*Brassica juncea*) "Green-in-Snow"

SAVE ENERGY THE EASY WAY

Why save energy? Most domestic energy supplies use fossil fuels (oil, coal, and gas), but burning these to create power produces carbon dioxide—one of the main greenhouse gases. So, by saving energy in our homes, we can help to minimize climate change.

Saving energy is easy. It can involve as little as turning off a light switch, to investing in house insulation and energy-efficient appliances. Since we pay for every unit of energy we use, saving energy also saves money.

Simple home improvements

Around 40 percent of the heat in a typical home is lost through the walls and the roof, so make sure that yours are insulated, if possible. Loft insulation is quick to install and reduces heating bills—the greenest type available is made

from sheep's fleece. Fitting an insulating jacket around your hot water heater will also help, or think about upgrading to a condensing boiler that can save a third on your heating bills.

Turn off any lights you are not using. It is a myth that leaving lights on uses less energy than "warming them up" and this is not true for any modern bulbs. Energy-efficient light bulbs use about a quarter of the electricity and last eight times longer than conventional bulbs.

Buy energy-efficient appliances: by changing to more efficient models you can save up to 33 percent every year on electricity and gas bills. Appliances now come with an Energy Star rating to help you choose the most efficient model.

Small changes that make a big difference

■ Turn off the TV and other appliances left on standby mode and unplug cell phone chargers: eight percent of electricity used at home is wasted by equipment on standby.

■ Put lids on your pans while you are cooking and choose the right size pans for the stovetop burners. Heating beyond the pan edge just warms air and wastes energy.

■ Use the washing machine only when you have a full load. Washing at 104°F (40°C) instead of 140°F (60°C) uses a third less electricity.

■ Open the doors of sunny rooms to allow the warm air to circulate through your home.

■ Close your drapes in winter to keep out cold draughts.

■ Dry clothes outside on a sunny day, rather than using the tumble dryer.

■ Don't overfill the kettle; boil the amount of water you need.

■ Use scrunched newspaper to keep your freezer packed.

■ Turn the temperature thermostat down by 2°F (1°C) to reduce your heating consumption by about ten percent.

■ Nearly 70 percent of the energy we use in our homes is used for heating rooms. Check that your furnace is running efficiently and have it serviced once a year.

■ Keep your fridge running efficiently by cleaning dust off the condenser coils at the back.

■ Sign up with a green energy supplier.

Energy facts

● Increasingly high levels of greenhouse gases are trapping heat in the atmosphere that would otherwise escape into space. This extra heat is causing the world's climates to change. Energy efficiency is the quickest, cheapest, and cleanest way to reduce greenhouse gas emissions, and to extend the world's energy supplies.

● When you turn on an ordinary incandescent light bulb, only 10% of the electricity used is turned into light. The other 90% is wasted as heat.

● One energy-efficient light bulb will save up to $14 and around 88 lb (40 kg) of carbon dioxide every year.

● If every household in the US changed to energy-efficient light bulbs, enough energy would be saved to power the lighting in ten million homes for a year.

● You can calculate how much energy your household uses (your "carbon footprint") at various websites.

SHOP ETHICALLY

Every purchase you make has either a direct or an indirect effect on your own health, on human and animal welfare, and on the environment. By asking yourself a few questions before you buy anything, you can effectively improve all of these situations and know that your impact on the world as a consumer has been a positive one. Ultimately, this way of shopping may also help you to improve your own quality of life.

Before making a purchase, ask yourself the following questions:

■ Where has the item come from?

■ How and who made the product? Were they treated fairly?

■ How long will you use the item for, and then can you recycle it? Or will it simply end up sitting in a landfill site for the next century or so?

■ How many miles has it had to travel before reaching you? Is there a less polluting alternative?

■ Is it truly fresh? What is keeping it looking so fresh?

Changing the way you shop could not be easier, as there are plenty of interesting and enjoyable ways of doing it.

Check out the label Don't trust a label just because the word "fresh" has been written in bright, bold letters across the product, for example. Find out more about what each labeling scheme is actually regulating, and then make your choice accordingly.

Buy organic Farmers registered as organic producers are allowed to use just seven natural pesticides on a restricted basis, as opposed to commercial farmers who can use up to 450 pesticides. It is now generally acknowledged that these large combinations of chemicals carry all sorts of health risks, as well as damaging soil structure and wildlife. Different

Unethical practices

- More energy is used in packaging many foods than in the foods themselves.

- The average item on sale in a supermarket has been transported at least 1,000 miles (1,609 km).

- The distribution of 2 lb 2 oz (1 kg) of apples air-freighted from New Zealand to the UK creates its own weight in CO_2 emissions.

- Conventional cotton farming is responsible for 25% of the world's total pesticide use.

- The majority of the non-organic fruit, vegetable, and bread samples tested in the US has been found to contain traces of pesticides.

- 99% of the world's coffee is not fairly traded. Millions of growers still receive less than 1% of the price we pay in shops and coffee bars.

- More than one in four of all fish caught are thrown back dead into the sea—about 27 million tons a year.

countries have varying regulations, so it's worth finding out about different regulatory boards and sticking to those that you recognize. Organic food usually tastes much better, too.

Buy seasonal Look out for vegetable box schemes or small producers who advertise on the internet. Buying seasonal food means that you'll be eating the freshest, tastiest fruit and vegetables available; a strawberry eaten in the winter never tastes quite as good as one eaten in the summer.

Buy local where possible Find out where your local farmers' markets are located. Supporting your own farming industry is crucial to sustaining local communities and reducing food miles. Without our farmers and small independent stores, we won't have such a choice in how we shop or what we eat.

Buy sustainably harvested fish Fish are being taken from the oceans faster than they can reproduce, causing problems for the sea's natural ecosystems. If trends continue, it is estimated that by 2050, we will run out of edible fish. Only buy fish that has been caught by an environmentally responsible fishery, such as those certified by the Marine Stewardship Council (MSC), or that has been farmed organically.

Choose fair trade Fairly traded goods ensure that growers get a fair price for their produce, enabling them to gain economic self-sufficiency and security.

Buy recycled The more demand there is for recycled goods, the more the market will provide them. Look out for recycled options on everyday purchases such as toilet paper, glassware, and garbage bags.

Season	Vegetables in season	Fruit in season
Winter	Beets, cabbages, carrots, celeriac, celery, chicory, endive, greens, kale, leeks, onions, parsnips, potatoes, pumpkins, and squashes, sprouts, turnips	Pears, rhubarb
Spring	Cabbages, cauliflowers, chicory, greens, leeks, lettuce, purple sprouting broccoli, radishes, watercress	Rhubarb
Summer	Artichokes, asparagus, beets, broccoli, cabbages, carrots, cauliflowers, chard, cucumbers, fennel, garlic, green beans, lettuce, new potatoes, peas, radishes, rocket, spinach, sweetcorn, tomatoes, watercress, zucchini,	Apples, apricots, blackcurrants, blueberries, cherries, loganberries, plums, redcurrants, strawberries, white currants
Fall	Beets, broccoli, cabbages, carrots, cauliflowers, celeriac, celery, chard, fennel, kale, leeks, onions, peppers, and chilies, potatoes, pumpkins, and squashes, spinach, sweetcorn, tomatoes, turnips, zucchini.	Blackberries, blueberries, raspberries, apples, pears, plums.

GROW POTS OF HERBS INDOORS

With a sunny window sill and the right choice of plants, you can create your own mini herb garden indoors and have a constant supply of fresh leaves to flavor your favorite dishes.

Any herb grown indoors needs to be positioned in good natural light. Some herbs, such as basil and thyme, need maximum sunlight and so do best on a south-facing windowsill. Here you could group together individual pots of basil, chives, oregano, thyme, and salad burnet for year-round snipping. Herbs such as parsley and winter savory cope well on cooler windowsills.

Many herbs are easy to grow from seed, although some are tricky to germinate, such as parsley and sage, which are best bought as young plants from a nursery or garden center (supermarket plants tend to be less robust). You can keep perennial herbs going right through the year by watering and feeding them carefully. Annuals, such as basil, should provide leaves for picking throughout the summer and into fall. Keep them well-watered, but avoid waterlogging. For a good, bushy plant, keep snipping off the growing tips to use in dishes, and don't allow your herbs to flower.

Grow herbs from seed

Seeds need water, light, and a constant, minimum temperature (check on the seed packet for details) to germinate. Most are best sowed in early spring.

Sow the seeds in seed trays or modules filled with good quality seed compost. Check the seed packets for sowing depths—fine seeds are usually sowed on the soil surface, larger ones should be covered with perlite (light natural granules) or soil.

Keep the soil moist, but not wet, and somewhere light and warm, such as on a window sill or in a propagator with a vented lid. Check the tray regularly as the seeds usually germinate quickly, in 10–14 days.

When the first seedlings appear, turn the tray or propagator around once a day if it is on a window sill. This keeps the shoots from bending toward the light.

Transfer the seedlings to their final pot when they have formed their second set of leaves. Make sure the pot has a drainage hole, add a layer of crocks or pebbles to the bottom, then top up with multi-purpose soil mixed with grit or horticultural sand. If you've used modules, squeeze out each seedling separately, hold it by the leaves and replant in the filled pot. Lever out seedlings from a seed tray with a stick and replant in the same way.

Tips for growing indoor herbs

- To keep the plant compact and encourage new growth, keep picking the leaves.

- Feed plants regularly with liquid plant food, such as seaweed.

- To keep the air humid on hot days, stand herbs with soft leaves on a tray of damp pebbles or spray them with a fine mist of water.

- If your herbs are positioned on a south-facing window sill, they may need to be shaded from the scorching midday sun.

- Avoid draughts and extremes of temperature.

Herbs for summer

Parsley (*Petroselinum crispum*)

Sweet basil (*Ocimum basilicum*)

Coriander (*Coriandrum sativum*)

Summer savory (*Satureja hortensis*)

Sweet marjoram (*Origanum majorana*)

Salad burnet (*Sanguisorba minor*)

Year-round herbs

Prostrate rosemary (*Rosemarinus officinalis* "Prostratus" *Group*)

Oregano (*Origanum vulgare*)

Winter savory (*Satureja montana*)

Mint (*Mentha spicata*)

Sage (*Salvia officinalis*)

Chives (*Allium schoenoprasum*)

Thyme (*Thymus vulgaris*)

Choose your culinary herbs

Pungent herbs, such as marjoram, rosemary, thyme, and sage, can add color and flavor to marinades and dishes as they cook. Delicate flavored herbs, such as parsley and chives, impart the most flavor and fragrance when sprinkled over hot and cold dishes.

Rosemary
Strong, refreshing taste that gives flavor to meat, fish, bread, and oils.

Parsley
Delicate flavor best used uncooked as a garnish sprinkled over dishes.

Thyme
An essential ingredient in bouquet garnis, stews, and casseroles. Use sparingly.

Sage
Herb with a distinctive flavor often used in stuffings for pork and chicken.

Chives
Mild herb that is best used uncooked. Sprinkle over salads and soups.

Mint
Fresh, clean tasting herb. Use in drinks, and savory, and sweet dishes.

Basil
Spicily fragrant leaves that lift the flavor of sauces, salads, and soups.

Oregano
Use sparingly in savory dishes and sauces.

BATHE USING PURE PRODUCTS

A plain vegetable soap is the best way to clean your body, as commercial products—body washes, bath foams and gels, and bubble baths—may include harsh detergents that strip the natural protective oils from your skin. But this doesn't mean that bathtime needs to be boring.

You can use any number of delicious organic essential oils to fragrance your bath. To help them disperse in the water, mix four to ten drops of your chosen oil with one tablespoon (½ fl oz/15 ml) of milk first: the fat in two percent or whole milk acts as a carrier to help distribute the oils evenly around the bath. For the greatest benefit, choose essential oils that match your skin type *(right)*.

If you want something a little more exotic, consider a fragrant mineral bath. Add a generous handful of Epsom salts and a few drops of your favorite essential oil (mixed with milk, as above) to the water while the bath is running. Epsom salts can be purchased at any drugstore for a fraction of the cost of name brand bath salts, which are essentially the same thing. Soaking your body in the salts encourages your skin to release accumulated toxins, and can help relieve tired muscles. So, in addition to being pleasant and safe to use, Epsom salts are therapeutic as well. For a bit of bathtime fizz, add a handful of baking soda to the bath at the same time.

Essential oils to match your skin type

Greasy skin
Lavender, orange, lemon, neroli, cypress, ylang-ylang, bergamot.

Normal skin
Palma rosa, geranium, lavender, Roman chamomile, jasmine, neroli, ylang ylang, frankincense, sandalwood, patchouli.

Sensitive skin
Geranium, lavender, German chamomile

Dry or damaged skin
Geranium, lavender, German chamomile, Roman chamomile, clary sage, myrrh.

Stay safe naturally

If you prefer to buy your bath products, make sure they are organic. Encourage your local stores to sell safer products and learn to read and understand the label. Avoid any products that contain the following ingredients:

- Sodium lauryl sulfate
- Cocamidopropl betaine
- Color (indicated by the letters CI, followed by a number)
- Parfum

MAKE FLAVORED OILS & VINEGARS

Oils and vinegars infused with herbs or fruit add a splash of color and a burst of flavor to salads, marinades, and sauces. And if you grow your own herbs, this is a great way to use them.

Good herbs for oils are thyme, oregano, sage, fennel, basil, and rosemary. Infused oils have the potential to support the growth of harmful bacteria, so follow the procedures listed carefully.

Suitable herbs for vinegars include dill, mint, thyme, and rosemary. Vinegars made with berries give a sweet, delicate flavor; try nasturtiums and roses, too.

Thyme & lemon oil

Ingredients
2 tablespoons fresh thyme leaves
Zest of 2 lemons
1 pint (570 ml) light olive oil

Method
■ In a food processor, blend the thyme and lemon zest with half the olive oil until the mixture is well blended.

■ Pour into a wide-mouthed jar, fill up with the remaining oil, and secure the lid tightly.

■ Leave in a cool, dark place for three days. Shake once a day for the first two days to increase the flavor of the oil. On the third day, allow the herbs to settle. On the fourth day, strain the mixture through a funnel lined with a coffee filter.

■ Refrigerate the flavored oil and use within three weeks.

Variation
Sage & orange oil
Use 3 tablespoons of fresh sage leaves and the zest of 2 oranges.

Rosemary, garlic & chilli oil

Ingredients

1 sprig (6 in/ 15 cm) fresh rosemary
4 cloves garlic
1–2 chili peppers (according to taste)
½ teaspoon chili powder
1 pint (570 ml) light olive oil

Method

■ Bruise the rosemary sprig with the end of a
wooden rolling pin.

■ Cut the garlic cloves in half.

■ Cut the chili pepper in half lengthwise.

■ Put the rosemary, garlic, chili pepper, and
chili powder into a clear 1 pint (570 ml) glass
bottle with a screw top.

■ Pour in the olive oil, secure the lid, shake
well, and refrigerate for two days before using.
Keep the bottle stored in the fridge and use
within one week.

Variation
Basil & garlic oil

Replace the rosemary with a handful of fresh
basil, gently bruised in the same way. Omit the
chili pepper and powder.

Raspberry vinegar

Ingredients

½ cup (110 g) raspberries

2 cups (570 ml) white wine vinegar

Method

■ Push the raspberries into a glass bottle, pour over the vinegar, and fasten the lid.

■ Allow to stand in a cool, dark place for at least two weeks, shaking gently daily, before using.

■ Strain the berries out of the vinegar after two weeks if you wish, or leave them in.

Uses

Sprinkle the raspberry vinegar on fruit salads, or use as part of a salad dressing or with chicken.

Variation

Elder vinegar

Use three heads of elderberries: remove the berries from their cluster and lightly crush first.

Rose vinegar

Ingredients

4 dark, perfumed rose heads with the petals removed

2 cups (570 ml) cider vinegar

Method

■ Place the petals in a glass jar with a tight-fitting lid.

■ Pour over the cider vinegar.

■ Fasten the lid securely and leave to macerate for two weeks in a cool, dark place.

■ Strain and bottle.

Uses

1 teaspoon of rose vinegar ½ cup (100 ml) water makes a refreshing, uplifting drink. Use also as a skin rinse for toning and energizing skin, or to lightly flavor fruit or cream dishes.

Nasturtium vinegar

Ingredients

6 nasturtium flowers

12 nasturtium seeds

6 nasturtium leaves

2 cups (570 ml) cider vinegar

Method

■ Place all the ingredients in a glass jar and fasten with a tightly fitting lid.

■ Leave to macerate for one week in a cool, dark place.

■ Strain and bottle.

Uses

Nasturtiums add a sharp, peppery bite to vinegar. Use to dress winter salads of potato, red cabbage, and celeriac.

SUPPORT LOCAL BUSINESSES

Air-freighting fresh produce has more than trebled in the past 20 years and, if the current shopping trends continue, we may soon arrive at a point where we'll have to rely on foreign imports for most of our everyday goods. Why not support local businesses by buying their seasonal free-range and organic produce, and help to reduce the environmental impact of imported food?

For those of us whose principle concern is our own or our children's health—but who are not and don't wish to be experts on nutrition—buying organic food is the easiest option. The organic standard, which requires a certification symbol or number on all organic produce, offers a genuine safety net, a basic protection against the worst of industrial food production.

For people who also care about fairness—fair and safe recompense for the producers of our daily foods—fair trade offers another basic standard. There are all kinds of reasons for this need for fair trading, the main one being that there are currently no laws to protect farmers. Large grocery stores can place whatever demands they want on farmers, who have to comply. And, at a time when concern about global warming has never been more widespread, these stores are importing goods that, traditionally, were produced seasonally and more locally.

Simple ways to buy locally

By buying direct from the producers themselves wherever possible, you can recompense them fairly for their work. The best way to do this is to shop as locally as you can.

Box schemes Boxes of freshly grown seasonal vegetables and fruit that are sent directly to your home from the farmer or supplier. Most schemes in operation use locally grown produce from small farms, where the emphasis is on flavor and quality.

Local farmers' markets
Usually sited outdoors, these increasingly popular markets are one of the best ways to shop, as they offer masses of variety. They also give you a chance to meet the people who have produced what you are going to eat.

Small specialist shops
These independent shops provide a more pleasurable shopping experience than the fridge- and freezer-humming environments of supermarkets. The vendors invariably have a much better knowledge of the different products on sale.

Local food makes perfect sense

While fair standards, buying organic and reducing the number of miles your food travels before it is consumed are all important reasons to shop ethically, if you believe in the value of choosing what you eat, and you care how it has been produced, then it's vital to support local farmers, shops and suppliers. In this way you can contribute to an increase in local market pressure on farmers to provide a greater diversity of locally produced food. There are, after all, only so many potatoes a local market can sell. And by diversifying their farms, farmers are necessarily moving to a more sustainable system of farming that will help to nourish the soil for generations to come.

The provenance of food

Most of the "nasties"—pesticides, fertilizers, antibiotics and hormones—used by commercial producers are designed to enable them to keep crops and animals in unnatural conditions. Diverse, free-range, small-scale farming techniques, on the other hand, automatically remove the need for these artificial props, and the worry that we might unknowingly be consuming harmful chemical residues. Free-range products bought locally can, therefore, be just as safe as organic produce that may have come from further away—with the advantage that you know where it has come from, and how it was grown or reared.

Facts on imported produce

● Air freighting is the fastest-growing form of food transportation.

● Per kilometre, air freighting releases 50 times more CO_2 into the atmosphere than sea freighting, and ten times more CO_2 than trucks transporting goods by road.

● A kiwi fruit creates five times its own weight in CO_2 emissions when flown across the world.

● Although the UK could meet over 70% of its eating needs by using food produced in that country, currently half of all the food consumed there is imported.

● In 2005, the US exported just under $42,000 million of goods to China, but imported over $240,000 million of goods—which represents a huge increase over the past 20 years.

CLEAN WITHOUT HARSH CHEMICALS

Most of us are in the habit of buying our cleaning products in the supermarket, so when we start to look for alternatives, we usually turn back to the same supermarket shelves, where genuinely green alternatives are often pretty scarce. Why not break the habit and try making your own? The simplest ingredients from your kitchen are often all that is needed for the majority of household cleaning jobs.

Baking soda A versatile product that is safe enough to drink (it's a common heartburn remedy) and brush your teeth with (it has a gentle whitening action). Used dry, or mixed with water and a tiny squirt of dishwashing liquid, it works as a disinfectant and mild abrasive that can remove hardened dirt and grease without scratching surfaces. It also softens water, so helping your other cleaners (including laundry detergents) clean and rinse off more effectively.

Vinegar Also known as acetic acid, vinegar is a mild acid that cuts though grease, disinfects, and discourages mold. Useful for cleaning glass and tiles and removing the coffee or tea stains on cups. It is also an efficient air freshener.

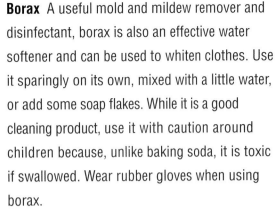

Borax A useful mold and mildew remover and disinfectant, borax is also an effective water softener and can be used to whiten clothes. Use it sparingly on its own, mixed with a little water, or add some soap flakes. While it is a good cleaning product, use it with caution around children because, unlike baking soda, it is toxic if swallowed. Wear rubber gloves when using borax.

Soap Real soap is made from natural products such as vegetable oils and animal fats. It is an effective cleaning agent that biodegrades quickly and has a minimal impact on the environment. Second best is an environmentally friendly dishwashing liquid.

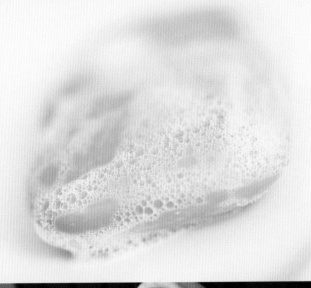

Microfiber cleaning cloths The basic purpose of detergents is to bring more water—one of the most efficient solvents in the world—into contact with whatever surface you are cleaning. Microfibers, which are finer than human hair and have amazing absorbency, effectively do the same thing. Used as directed they will leave most surfaces clean and dry. The most effective cloths have densely packed fibers.

DRY YOUR OWN HERBS

Harvest and dry your own herbs while they are full of the aromatic oils that give them their intense flavors, and have a supply for the kitchen for the rest of the year.

Some herbs, such as rosemary, thyme, and bay, can be picked right through the winter, but most herbs either die down or are annuals and go to seed. The best way to preserve leaves is by drying them (delicate leaves such as basil, chervil, dill, and tarragon are better frozen). The best time is when the plant has formed its flower buds, but before the flowers have opened. This will vary from plant to plant, so keep an eye on your herbs, and don't be shy about asking friends or relatives to snip off a few stalks from their plant if you spot a herb you don't have.

Harvest the leaves on a dry day, preferably in the morning before it gets too hot: strong sun causes leaf oils to evaporate.

Cut whole stalks using scissors or pruning shears and dry as quickly as possible to keep the full flavor and color. A warm (but not too hot) airy room is ideal for drying them.

Dry on a tray or wire rack, or on a piece of muslin stretched over and attached to a wooden frame, which you can make yourself. Take the leaves off the stalk, spread them out in a single layer, and turn over occasionally as they are drying.

Once the leaves have become crispy and brittle, crumble them up, pour them into glass storage jars, and label. Stored in a cool, dark cabinet, they should keep their flavor for about a year.

Drying tips

● If the herbs still have moisture in them when they are put into jars, they will go moldy. Check the lids for the first few days and if you see moisture on the inside, tip out the herbs and dry off fully.

● Drying intensifies the flavor of herbs, making them three to four times more potent than fresh ones, so use them more sparingly in your cooking.

● Good for drying: sage, rosemary, bay, mint, lovage, thyme, oregano, summer savory.

CHECK THE LABEL

Indoor air pollution is a problem on the rise. Since most of us spend 90 percent of our time indoors—in homes, offices, and schools—pollutants can contribute substantially to poor health.

The air indoors can be compromised by any number of things, from the presence of a smoker to the use of formaldehyde-laden particleboard furnishings. But according to the US Environmental Protection Agency (EPA), a primary cause of indoor pollution is the use of conventional household cleaners.

Cleaning products

The problem is that in order to fulfil the increasingly ambitious claims for their products, manufacturers rely on combinations of chemicals that can be harsh and highly toxic. Many of these products easily evaporate or give off gases that can contaminate the air indoors. If a cleaner can instantly strip a kitchen tile of years of accumulated grease, what might it do to your skin or your body's cells if you happen to breathe it in, or to the natural environment?

Since household cleaners are not required to carry full ingredients labels, you will have to look for "signal words" that help to identify the kind of cleaner you are using. This table *(right)* identifies the names of some ingredients that may be listed in toxic products.

Check if it's toxic

You'll know a product is toxic if one of the following words, or something similar, is included on its label:

Hazardous

Corrosive

Inflammable

Warning

Caution

Danger

Irritant

Product	Substance	Health effects
Air fresheners, furniture polishes	Parfum	Linked to asthma, nausea, mood changes, depression, skin irritation, lethargy, irritability, memory lapses.
All-purpose cleaners	Alcohol (incl. ethanol, methanol, isopropanol)	Nausea and vomiting if swallowed. Also found in dishwashing liquid, glass, and window cleaners.
	Propylene glycol	Irritant and immunotoxin. Also found in dishwashing detergents.
	Sodium tripolyphosphate	Skin, eye, and lung irritant. Also found in laundry detergents.
Bathroom & toilet cleaners	Chlorine	Eye, skin, and lung irritant. Major cause of poisonings in children. Also found in disinfectants, dishwasher powders.
	Paradichlorobenzenes	Irritates eyes, nose, central nervous system. Also found in mildew control sprays, room deodorizers.
	Phenol	Extremely dangerous; suspected carcinogen; fatal if taken internally. Also found in disinfectants.
Degreasers	Butyl cellosolve	Liver, kidney, central nervous system damage. Also found in all-purpose cleaners, window cleaners.
Furniture polish	Formaldehyde	Highly toxic; known carcinogen. Also found in all-purpose cleaners, dishwashing liquid, disinfectants, deodorizing sprays.
Glass & window cleaners	Ammonia	Fatal when swallowed. Also found in floor cleaners, furniture, and metal polishes, disinfectants.
Limescale & rust removers	Hydrochloric acid	Corrosive, eye and skin irritant. Also found in toilet cleaners, metal polishes.
Metal & shoe polishes	Nitrobenzene	Causes skin discoloration, shallow breathing, vomiting, birth defects, and death.
Oven & drain cleaners	Lye (sodium hydroxide)	Severe damage to stomach and esophagus if swallowed. Also found in bathroom and toilet cleaners.
	Naphtha	Depresses the central nervous system.
Spot removers, dry-cleaning fluids	Trichloroethane	Damages liver and kidneys, narcotic. Also found in metal polishes, fabric cleaners, degreasers.

REDUCE, REUSE & RECYCLE

The average person in the West throws out their own body weight in garbage every three months. Disposing of our domestic waste requires landfill space, increases the number of garbage trucks on our roads, and creates pollution problems, so reducing the amount we throw away makes sense.

We are all being encouraged to recycle now, but recycling is only one way that we can minimize the garbage we produce. Instead, think the "three Rs:" reduce, reuse, and recycle.

Reduce your waste

Reducing the amount of garbage we create is one of the best things we can do for the environment. Nearly all our waste comes from the things we buy, so reducing waste doesn't start at the garbage cans, but at the stores. Almost 75 percent of the garbage from an average household is due to packaging.

- Choose products with the minimum amount of packaging.
- Buy your fruit and vegetables loose.
- Choose products with recyclable packaging.
- Buy in bulk packs; one large pack uses less packaging than two small units.
- Beware child-oriented packaging and snack sizes. Make your own lunch box portions and wrap them in wax paper or reusable bags or containers.

Try the three Rs with shopping bags

Reduce

- Don't use new plastic bags every time you shop. Instead, take a couple of strong jute or fabric bags with you—or use a backpack, which is the best way to carry the load and maintain your posture. Spread the weight between the two bags and hold a bag in each hand for balance.

Reuse

- Keep a few plastic bags in your purse or in the car so that you can reuse them each time you go shopping.

- Reuse plastic bags in your wastebaskets instead of always buying new liners.

- Alternatively, take along any plastic bags you can't reuse to your local thrift store, which should be able to reuse them easily for you.

Recycle

- Only when your old plastic bags are worn out should you dispose of them. The best way to do this is at recycling collection points (which can now be found outside many supermarkets and stores).

Reuse household items

Reusing items means giving them another lease of life before discarding or recycling them.

■ Refill empty mineral water bottles with tap water. Wash the bottles regularly to prevent a build-up of germs.

■ Take any unwanted clothes to thrift shops, garage sales, or churches.

■ Children usually outgrow their clothes before they wear them out. Why not meet with other parents to give away or swap your children's clothes?

■ Local communities are often in need of paint, wallpaper, and other excess household items. Ask your city government about what and how you can give unwanted items away.

■ Be inventive with your empty containers! Use plastic or metal containers to store kitchen or household items, or to grow herbs, flowers, or seeds.

Recycle to reduce energy consumption

The terms reusing and recycling are often confused, but recycling generally means to re-form something. Recycled paper, for example, is first washed free of ink, then pulped and squeezed out into new sheets. Certain plastics are recycled into carpet fibers, garden furniture, agricultural pipes, garbage bags, clothes pegs, and so on. Metal and glass are recycled by melting the old material in a furnace and remolding it. Interestingly, recycling an aluminum can uses only five percent of the energy it would take to make a new can from mined aluminum ore, and the energy saved is enough to power a TV for two hours. If you don't have a recycling cart that is collected regularly by your city, use your own separate cans or boxes to recycle glass, paper, and plastic, if possible, and take them to your local recycling depot when they're full. Other household waste can also be recycled *(right)*.

So recycling is better than using new—and reusing is even better—but reducing our waste in the first place is the greenest option. Remember, recycling industries only exist if there is a market for their products. So buy recycled goods wherever you can.

What can you recycle?

■ **Paper and cardboard** Recycling paper doesn't just save trees, it saves significant amounts of water and electricity, too.

■ **Glass** Glass can be recycled indefinitely.

■ **Plastic** Many plastic bottles are now made of recyclable plastic. Those with a recycling symbol and the numbers 1 and 2 are most commonly accepted for recycling.

■ **Textiles** Charities can make money by selling donated, worn clothes to various industries.

■ **Batteries** The toxic metals in batteries can contaminate groundwater. Take used batteries to appropriate recycling centers so that the metals can be retrieved.

■ **Metal** Aluminum from soda cans and tinfoil is currently the most valuable of all recyclable waste.

■ **Compost** If you have an outdoor space, compost your kitchen and garden waste.

BAKE BREAD

If you bake your own organic bread, you have complete control over the ingredients you use. You can use different flours to make a variety of flavored and textured breads, but wheat flour and a cultivated yeast will make the simplest of loaves. Try to source a local stoneground wheat flour, or use a granary flour.

Wheat contains the proteins glutenin and gliadin which, when combined with water and kneaded, produce gluten—elastic strands that trap the carbon dioxide made by the yeast and cause the bread to rise. It is impossible to give precise instructions for making bread, as different flours absorb variable amounts of liquid. The rising times will vary too, depending on the warmth of the room. In the following recipe, you may need to add more water; the ideal dough is soft, but firm, in texture and you should be able to knead it easily.

Wholemeal bread (makes three loaves)

Ingredients

3 lb (1.35 kg) wholemeal flour

1 teaspoon salt

1 oz (45 g) yeast

1 teaspoon honey

2 cups (850 ml) tepid water

1 lb (3 x 450 g) bread tins.

Method

■ Put the flour and salt into a bowl. Make a well in the center.

■ Crumble in the yeast, add the honey, and ½ cup (100 ml) of water, sprinkle flour over the well and leave in a warm place for 15 minutes.

■ Slowly mix in the rest of the water until you have a sticky, but quite firm, dough.

■ Turn out and knead gently for about 10 minutes until smooth. Put the dough in a clean bowl, cover, and leave in a warm place until it doubles in size (about 1 hour).

■ Turn the dough out and divide into three. Shape the dough and place in oiled bread tins.

■ Cover with a cloth and leave for at least 40 minutes until the dough rises above the rim of the tin. Preheat the oven to 425°F/ 220°C.

■ Put the tins in the oven. After 40 minutes, remove. Tip out each loaf. Rap the base of a loaf with your knuckles; if it doesn't sound hollow, bake it for ten more minutes without the tin.

CHOOSE NATURAL DIAPERS

When disposable diapers were first sold, they seemed like a great idea. Moms said goodbye to washing soiled cloth diapers and tossed the new plastic-lined disposables into the garbage. We now know that more natural diapers are much better for your baby's skin, and for the environment.

Disposable diapers lined in plastic are made from synthetic fibers that contain deodorizing chemicals, bleaches, and highly toxic dioxins, which are now known to be harmful to a baby's skin and to the environment. It is estimated that a plastic disposable diaper may take up to 500 years to biodegrade.

Kinder alternatives

Now the pendulum is swinging back to using cloth diapers and biodegradable disposables. Cloth diapers can be made from cotton, wool, silk, hemp, and even bamboo fibers. Fitted cloth diapers that are easier to use are now available. They have velcro fastenings and disposable, flushable inner linings that make them just as waterproof and a great deal kinder to your baby's skin. They are also more absorbent than plastic diapers.

There are also new types of disposables available, which are made from more natural, chlorine-free, biodegradeable constituents that don't make use of super absorbent gels *(right)*, and are free from perfumes and other harmful chemicals.

The average baby will get through approximately 5,000 diapers. Advantages of using diapers made from natural fibers include:

No chemicals Cloth and biodegradable diapers contain no harmful bleaches, dyes, and hormone-disrupting chemicals. Plastic-lined disposables contain a super-absorbent gelling material known as sodium polyacrylate, which can soak up 30 times its own weight in liquid. This gel releases an estrogenlike chemical close to the baby's skin.

Less diaper rash The absorbent gel material in plastic disposables can make a diaper feel dry even when it is wet. As a result, parents may be tempted to leave their baby in a diaper for longer. This exposes your baby to ammonia, which urine produces as it breaks down, and which can irritate skin and produce diaper rash.

Economy Washed carefully, as you would any other item of clothing, cotton diapers should last you through two (or more) children. Cloth diapers can be washed and reused up to 200 times, and then used as lint-free cleaning rags.

Preserving the earth's resources The manufacturing process involved in producing biodegradable disposable diapers does far less harm to the environment than plastic disposables because no bleaching agents are used.

The facts on plastic disposables

● Every year in the US alone, up to 20 billion disposable diapers are sent to landfill sites. It is estimated that diaper waste comprises up to 2% of all household waste.

● Viruses in soiled disposable diapers can survive for over two weeks, and run-off from landfills containing disposable diapers can contaminate groundwater supplies.

● Plastic disposables use 3½ times more total energy, 8 times more non-renewable materials, and 90 times more renewable materials than cloth diapers. They produce 60 times more solid waste and use 25% more land for growing the materials used in their manufacture.

FORAGE FOR WILD GREENS

If you don't have room for more than a couple of herbs or leafy vegetables in your window boxes, you can still enjoy herby soups, dishes of spinachlike greens, and salads with a selection of tangy leaves by collecting wild greens.

The leaves that you can gather in the wild won't have been "improved" or artificially fertilized; they will provide you with an array of different tastes and textures; and, of course, they're free. It may take you half a day of foraging to pick enough leaves for a soup or dish, but it's a wonderful way of getting to know the wild plants of an area and discover the tastes our ancestors enjoyed long before we bought our vegetables at supermarkets. You can find edible greens almost all year round and in all sort of places, from marshy spots to woods, grassy areas, hedgerows and even waste ground. Just make sure that you never strip an area bare or uproot plants.

Many wild plants are edible, but they have a much more bitter flavor than we're used to so try small amounts to start with. For example, the sharpness of dandelion leaves, picked before the flowers come out, is definitely an acquired taste. On the other hand, sweet cicely has sugary leaves that combine deliciously with stewed fruit.

Safe picking and eating

● Only pick a plant if you're 100% sure of what it is. Whether you're new to foraging or not, always take a couple of reliable botanical field guides with you.

● Don't pick from any areas that might have been sprayed with weedkiller or insecticide, or from the verges of heavily used roads.

● Don't pick discolored or withered leaves.

● If you have never eaten a particular plant before, try just a small amount the first time you eat it in case it disagrees with you.

Twelve of the best wild greens

1 **Chickweed** *(Stellaria media)*
A tender wild green, with a taste like corn salad, that can be picked all year except when frosty. Add to salads.

2 **Common nettle** *(Urtica dioica)*
Rich in vitamins A and C, the leaves are best picked young and cooked like spinach or made into a soup.

3 **Garlic mustard** *(Alliara petiolata)*
Pick a few young leaves from each plant. Finely chop them and add to salads for a mildly garlic flavor.

4 **Wild thyme** *(Thymus drucei)*
Pick when in flower and use raw to make a tisane, or in soups and cooked dishes. Milder than the cultivated varieties.

5 **Hairy bittercress** *(Cardamine hirsuta)*
The leaves of this plant have a sweet, tangy flavor and can be used in salads and sandwiches.

6 **Alexanders** *(Smyrnium olusatrum)*
The spicy young leaves can be added to salads, and the pinkish part of the stems can be boiled and eaten like asparagus.

7 **Garden sorrel** (*Rumex acetosa*)
The sharp-tasting leaves can be added to salads and cooked dishes.

8 **White watercress**
(*Rorippa nasturtium-aquaticum)*
This tastes just like the plants that are grown commercially. For a stronger flavor, pick the older, darker leaves, but make sure the plant grows in clean, fast flowing water.

9 **Good King Henry**
(*Chenopodium bonus-henricus*)
This is a perennial, which can be picked almost all year round and cooked like spinach or added to soups.

10 **Common hops** *(Humulus lupulus)*
Pick the young shoots and leaves in late spring and early summer. Add to soups and omelettes, or soak in salt water for an hour and blanch until tender.

11 **Lamb's quarters** (*Chenopodium album)*
This plant rapidly colonizes waste ground. The leaves are best cooked like spinach.

12 **Sweet fennel** (*Foeniculum vulgare)*
Cut the leaves early in the summer and add to fish dishes and potato salads.

NOURISH SKIN NATURALLY

The simpler your skincare regime, the better. Conventional skin creams and lotions can contain mixtures of 20 or more synthetic ingredients, many of which are of no direct benefit to your skin. Instead, they are necessary to hold mixtures of incompatible ingredients, such as oil and water, together and to extend the product's shelf life.

When you buy a conventional skin care product, you are buying a quick fix, something that may well produce a fast, temporary result—for instance, visible results in an hour—but which doesn't actually do anything to improve your skin in the long term.

Organic products tend to be much more straightforward mixtures that work in a different way. The organic plant-based ingredients tend to have higher levels of naturally occurring vitamins and trace elements of essential fatty acids—all the things that your skin needs to nourish and protect it.

As an alternative to mineral oil-based products, which are derived from petroleum, why not consider using simple, natural plant- or animal-based oils to maintain your skin's natural moisture balance? Many of these oils, such as jojoba and emu, are amazingly similar to the oils in human skin and as such are non-irritating, won't clog pores, and are deeply nourishing. Better still, they do the same job at a fraction of the price of commercial brands, and you'll have the advantage of knowing what you are using on your skin.

Choose organic products

If you still prefer to buy your skincare products, make sure that they are organic. Encourage your local shops to sell safer products and read and learn to understand the label. Avoid any skin products that contain these ingredients:

- Butylparaben (and other parabens)
- Parafinnum liquidum
- Cyclomethicone
- Parfum

Beneficial oils for your skin

Apply a small amount of your chosen oil with damp hands, or after bathing, to keep your skin soft and protected.

For younger skin
Apricot kernel oil

Coconut oil

Hemp seed oil

Wheat germ oil

Olive oil

For more mature skin
Avocado oil

Evening primrose oil

Rosa mosqueta oil

For any skin type
Almond oil

Cocoa butter

Emu oil

Jojoba

Squalene

Homemade scrub

Make a simple exfoliating scrub for your body or face by mixing a natural oil (olive oil is a good choice) with honey and sugar. If you have sensitive skin, use ground oatmeal instead of sugar for a gentler exfoliating action. Don't use exfoliating products too often: once a week is enough.

USE SAFER PEST CONTROLS AT HOME

Sharing our homes with rodents, insects, or other uninvited creatures can be unpleasant, and occasionally dangerous. But before you reach for the nearest commercial pesticide, try some safer alternatives.

Homeowners in the US use over one billion pounds of commercial pesticides each year. Often, though, the potential harm pests cause in the home is outweighed by the toxicity of the chemicals in these pesticide products: powders, for example, can irritate the lungs, even if the product is not labeled as toxic (it's important to note that you should always read the label of any pest control product). And not all creatures that come into our homes and yards are pests. Some, such as spiders, can be beneficial as they eat flies and mosquitoes, while wasps kill many garden pests.

Basic principles

The first rule of pest management is to avoid encouraging any pests in the first place. Seal all cracks and holes in walls or floors where mice or insects could enter (rodents won't chew through wire wool), and consider fitting screens over doors, windows, and vents.

Simple preventative measures

■ Keep food in tightly sealed jars or plastic boxes, not open packages.

■ Keep floors and surfaces clean—wipe up crumbs and sticky spills quickly.

■ Rinse food and drink containers before throwing them away or recycling them.

■ Keep your garbage cans covered and empty them regularly.

If these four simple, preventative measures don't work, try the following non-toxic or "least toxic" methods of killing or discouraging pests.

Ants

■ Stop ants from reaching pet food by placing the food bowl in a shallow container filled with soapy water, making a moat that the ants cannot cross.

■ Try crushing and sprinkling pennyroyal, sage, mint, thyme or bay leaves, paprika, or cinnamon across ant paths.

■ Boric acid and borate-based products are effective (a natural product, boric acid is far less toxic than chemical pesticides, but is mildly harmful if ingested so use it sparingly).

Clothes moths

■ Washing clothes at high temperature kills the eggs and larvae, or put wool clothes in a freezer for 72 hours.

■ Store clothes made from natural fibers in airtight bags.

■ Place sachets of lavender or cedarwood chips among stored clothes.

■ Pheromone traps will catch adult moths, but not the damage-causing grubs.

Mosquitoes

■ Protect yourself: use a spray bottle filled with ten drops of essential oil (try cedarwood, lemongrass, peppermint, citronella, or eucalyptus) and 4 fl oz (115 ml) of water.

■ Mosquitoes don't like breezes, so use a fan.

■ Sleep under a mosquito net.

■ Limit mosquito breeding places by keeping lids on containers holding water, emptying standing water from old flower pots, etc.

Herbal flea collar

1 untreated soft felt collar

Mix together:

2 teaspoons pure alcohol
1 tablespoon rosemary
essential oil
1 tablespoon lemon verbena
essential oil
1 tablespoon lavender
essential oil
1 tablespoon pennyroyal
essential oil
Oil of 4 garlic capsules

Soak the flea collar thoroughly
in the mixture, then dry. The
effect lasts for one month.

Rats & mice

■ There are many types of trap available. Some are lethal, others are humane, allowing you to release mice outdoors.

■ Pet cats keep mice down, terrier dogs may keep rats at bay.

Fleas

■ Use a flea comb on your pet. Drown any fleas you catch in soapy water.

■ Clean bedding and vacuum your home regularly.

■ Use essential oils to make a flea collar *(left)*.

Food moths

■ Some food moth grubs eat flour, cereals, and many other foods. Seal and throw away any contaminated food.

■ Grubs can even chew through packaging, so inspect unopened boxes.

■ The grubs can crawl up walls and into cracks before they pupate. Use a vacuum cleaner to get right into these spots.

■ The outdoor moths that fly into the house at night will not cause problems.

Cockroaches

■ Dust boric acid into the cracks where cockroaches shelter.

■ Diatomaceous earth is a dust that scratches the waterproof coat of cockroaches and other crawling insects, causing them to dry out and die.

House flies

■ Use fly screens made of chain links or beads in doorways.

■ Muslin covers prevent flies from settling on food.

■ Try hanging a sweet basil plant by a window or back door.

Homemade fly paper

Mix together equal parts by volume of sugar, golden syrup, and water. Boil the mixture until thick, stirring occasionally.

Leave to cool, then dip strips of brown packaging tape into the sticky mixture. Leave to dry outside for about 30 minutes.

Hang up with string. The flies will be attracted to, and trapped on, the sticky coating.

■ Fly-paper or sticky strips are effective. Homemade versions *(above)* won't give off toxic fumes or bad odors.

■ UV lights and electronic zappers work, but do use up energy.

Wasps

■ Don't leave sweet food or drinks out.

■ Buy a wasp trap, or make your own using a bottle or jar. Wasps like sweet food, so mix jam with water and a drop of detergent to bait your trap. The detergent helps to kill them.

■ Wasps in wasps' nests die over winter, so leave them alone if they are not bothering you.

GROW STRAWBERRIES IN A HANGING BASKET

Fill a hanging basket with strawberry plants, hang it somewhere sheltered and sunny, and enjoy pretty white flowers in early summer followed by lots of juicy red fruits. A hanging basket is an ideal way of growing strawberries, as it keeps the fruit off the ground and so is much less likely to suffer from pests (such as slugs) and diseases.

It's a good idea to line the basket with porous material—you could use sphagnum moss or coconut fiber.
■ Make up a mixture of potting soil with a couple of handfuls of vermiculite and some bonemeal forked into it, and fill the basket. For a large basket, buy five or six plants in the spring, plant them, and water well.

Once the plants start to grow, feed them with a liquid fertilizer that's high in potassium, such as tomato food, every 10–14 days. Keep well watered, and daily in hot weather.

When you've picked all the fruit, the plants will stop growing for a few weeks. Then in early fall, they will make more crowns again in preparation for the next year. You should be able to keep your plants going for three seasons before replacing them. Don't forget to refresh the potting soil every spring.

If you have space for another basket, you could propagate another batch of strawberry plants and get more berries the following year. Strawberries make new plantlets at the end of runners. Hang the second basket right next to the first one. In early fall lift up several of the runners from the main basket and lay the plantlets onto the soil of the second one. Pin down each runner with some galvanized wire.

After a few weeks when the new plants have rooted (gently tug to check), cut the runners that attach them to the mother plant.

Try tomatoes

If you are not a fan of strawberries, try growing cherry tomatoes instead. Varieties such as the red "Tumbler" or the yellow "Tumbling Tom Yellow" are ideal for hanging baskets.

● Use one plant in a small basket (10 in/ 25 cm diameter), three in a large basket.

● Use potting soil with a mixture of vermiculite and sand for drainage.

● Feed plants tomato fertilizer little and often.

● Water frequently, especially during hot weather. Make sure that the basket has good drainage, as waterlogging causes the fruit to split.

● Pick when ripe. At the end of the season, pick off the last tomatoes and ripen them indoors.

TRAVEL WISELY

Moving products and people around is an essential part of modern life, but many forms of transportation, plus the sheer scale of our transportation infrastructure, are causing problems to our health and environment.

Road traffic and air travel are the fastest-growing sources of the main greenhouse gas, carbon dioxide. Exhaust pollution can aggravate lung and breathing problems, and traffic accidents are all too common. Road traffic and aircraft noise can disrupt daily life, and roads and runways now cover miles of countryside. By changing some of our transportation decisions, however, we can not only reduce our impact on the planet, but improve our health, too.

Rather than driving everywhere in your car, try other options such as walking or cycling: a brisk 20 minute walk will give you a good aerobic work out, while people who cycle regularly typically have a fitness level equivalent to someone who is ten years younger.

Reduce your car usage

■ If everyone replaced just one roundtrip car trip per week with another form of travel, traffic on the roads would be reduced by more than ten percent.

■ If one of your regular trips is to drop off the kids at school because you have no regular school bus service, how about organizing a "walking bus" scheme, where two or more adults pick up children and escort them along a pre-arranged pedestrian route to school? Or, you can always carpool.

■ Think about organizing a carpool with your co-workers. Many companies now offer preferential parking or other incentives to discourage individual car commuting.

■ Plan to get as much as you can out of a car trip. One trip to undertake five tasks is better for the environment than five separate car trips.

Facts on travel

● Half of all car trips made are less than 2 miles (2.5 km).

● 60% of all car trips have only one person in the car.

● Globally, around 1.2 million people are killed in car accidents each year.

● An airplane creates three times more CO_2 and pollution than a train on distances less than 300 miles (500 km).

● Globally, aircraft generate more than 700 million tons of CO_2 per year.

● A passenger taking a long-haul return flight from the US to the UK produces as much CO_2 as a driver does driving in the UK for a year.

Tips for greener driving

Limit the use of air conditioning in your car, as it uses up more fuel.

Reduce the weight of your car by unloading any heavy items you won't need on the trip.

Drive with the windows up, and remove the roof rack if you aren't using it. This reduces drag and makes your fuel consumption more efficient.

Check that your tires are inflated to the correct tire pressure. For every 6psi the tire is underinflated, the fuel consumption increases by one percent.

Consider converting your car so that it can use biofuels, including ethanol. These fuels are much less polluting than gasoline, and are becoming increasingly available.

Keep your speed down It can cost you up to 25 percent more in fuel to drive at 70 mph (110 kph) compared to 50 mph (80 kph).

Harsh acceleration and braking can use up to 30 percent more fuel.

Avoid unnecessary revving or idling of the engine. It's more efficient to turn your engine off if you are stuck in a traffic jam.

A well-tuned engine improves a car's performance and limits fuel consumption.

Consider buying a small, efficient car for your everyday needs, and renting a larger car for longer trips when you need it. Driving a 12 mpg SUV rather than a 25 mpg car can waste more energy in one year than leaving the fridge door open for seven years.

Consider using a hybrid vehicle, which saves energy by using an electric battery as well as gasoline.

Thinking about a vacation?

Artificially cheap flights may make you feel that vacations on sunny coasts or short city breaks abroad are almost obligatory. But there are other options. You could:

● Take a train.

● Go by boat. A cruise is possibly the most relaxing start to any vacation.

● Explore your own state, region, or country and discover new areas.

Air travel

Aircraft release more than 600 million tons of the world's major greenhouse gas, carbon dioxide, into the atmosphere each year. They also release other greenhouse gases, including nitrogen oxides (NOx) and water vapor. These have a more significant effect on the climate when emitted at altitude than at ground level. Aircraft vapor trails, or contrails, can also encourage the formation of cirrus clouds. Both contrails and cirrus clouds warm the earth's surface, magnifying the global warming effect of aviation.

Although aircraft and engine technology is improving, this will not offset the projected growth in aircraft emissions. The only way to reduce aircraft greenhouse gas emissions is to fly less.

Hidden transportation costs

It isn't just the trips that you personally make that have an impact on the planet. The products you buy also have hidden transportation costs. Flying 2 lb 4oz (1 kg) of asparagus from California to the UK, for example, uses 900 times more energy than the local British equivalent, and food transportation is responsible for around a quarter of the semis on our roads.

Buy locally produced food wherever you can to help to reduce "food miles"—the total distance that food is transported from field to plate.

How efficient is your trip?

In terms of the amount of fossil fuels burned, cars and planes are very inefficient ways to travel. Buses and trains are much less polluting.

g carbon dioxide per passenger mile	
Train	45
Bus	48
Car	71
Plane	205
(short-haul flights)	

MAKE & FREEZE BABY FOODS

How and what we eat as babies and toddlers can have a huge influence on our long-term health. Poor nutrition in childhood has been shown to cause heart disease and diabetes in adults. Make the most of local seasonal fruit and vegetables and turn them into simple, nutritious meals for your child.

Frozen baby food has a better flavour than organic jars, and is preservative-free. Use small, sealable containers to fill the freezer with individual portions. Thaw them thoroughly before reheating and feeding them to your child. Always make smoothies fresh.

Zucchini & tomato scones

(from 12 months old)

If you freeze the scones, use within one month.

Ingredients

12 oz (350 g) all-purpose wholemeal flour

1 teaspoon baking powder

2 oz (50 g) butter

2 oz (50 g) zucchini, grated

2 sundried tomatoes, finely chopped

1 teaspoon fresh thyme, chopped

½ pint (275 ml) milk

Method

■ Put the flour and baking powder in a bowl. Rub in the butter.

■ Stir in the zucchini, tomatoes, thyme, and enough milk to make a manageable dough.

■ Roll out the dough until it is about ¾ in (2 cm) thick. Cut into rounds. Place on an oiled baking tray and bake for 12–15 minutes at 350°F/180°C.

Variation
Red pepper & olive scones

Use 1 finely diced red pepper and 8 black olives, pitted and finely chopped.

Herb mash

(from 8 months old)

Use a mix of whatever fresh herbs you have on hand—parsley, chives, fennel, and tarragon are all good choices. The garlic and beet mashes freeze well, but the herb mash doesn't.

Ingredients

2 large potatoes, washed and pricked
2 tablespoons fresh herbs, chopped
A knob of butter and a splash of olive oil

Method

■ Bake the potatoes in an oven at 425°F/220°C for about 1½ hours.

■ When cooked, split in half, scoop the potato into a bowl, and mash. Stir in the herbs, butter, and oil. If the mix is dry, add a little rice milk.

Variations

Garlic mash Omit the herbs. Soften 2 finely chopped cloves of garlic in the olive oil and butter before stirring into the mashed potato.

Beet mash Bake a beet at the same time as the potatoes. Skin the beet and mash it with the potato, or process to a purée first. The mixture should be soft enough without adding rice milk.

Carrot soup with ginger

(from 8 months old)

Both the carrot soup and the parsnip variation will freeze well. Use small containers with well-fitting lids and eat within one month of freezing. Served with a chunk of fresh bread, these soups make a satisfying supper for older children and adults, too.

Ingredients

2 tablespoons (50 g) butter

1½ lb (700 g) carrots, washed and chopped

1 medium onion, chopped

1 in (2.5 cm) cube fresh root ginger, grated

4 cups (1.2 liters) salt-free vegetable stock

Method

■ Melt the butter in a thick-bottomed pan, then stir in the chopped carrots and onion. Simmer gently for five minutes.

■ Stir in the grated ginger and cook for a further three minutes.

■ Add the stock and simmer, with the pan covered, for 15 minutes.

■ Cool slightly, then process the mixture in a blender until smooth.

Serve with a swirl of fresh yogurt or a sprinkling of freshly chopped parsley.

Variation

Parsnip soup with ginger Replace the carrots with 1½ lb (700 g) parsnips and cook according to the same method.

Barley & vegetable casserole

(from 10 months old)

This dish is delicious fresh or frozen.

Ingredients

2 tablespoons olive oil

2 cloves garlic, peeled and chopped

1 onion, diced

1 small parsnip, diced

1 medium carrot, diced

1 small celeriac, diced

½ cup (50 g) pot barley

2 cups (570 fl oz) salt-free vegetable stock

Method

■ Heat the oil in a thick-bottomed pan. Cook the garlic gently in the oil for a few minutes.

■ Add the vegetables and stir for two minutes, then add the barley and stock.

■ Bring to the boil, reduce the heat, and simmer gently for 40 minutes.

■ Mash lightly if required and serve.

Variation

Garbanzo bean & vegetable casserole Replace the pot barley with garbanzo beans which, if dried, need soaking for 24 hours before using.

Banana & raspberry smoothie

(from 8 months old)
None of these drinks are suitable for freezing.

Ingredients

1 banana, peeled, sliced, and frozen
1 large handful (1 cup/150 g) fresh raspberries
1 cup (230 ml) apple juice

Method

■ Put all the ingredients in a blender.
■ Cover and process on a low speed until smooth.
■ Pour the smoothie into a suitable container for your baby, decant the rest into a glass for yourself, and serve.

Variations

Banana & strawberry smoothie

Replace raspberries with strawberries.

Banana & blackberry smoothie

Replace raspberries with blackberries.

Fruit & protein smoothie For babies over 18 months, replace the apple juice with almond milk made by processing blanched almonds and water (in a ratio of 1:3) in a blender until very smooth.

CHOOSE NATURAL FACE & BODY PRODUCTS

It's important to use toiletries and cosmetics that are as pure as possible. There are literally hundreds of chemicals that go into conventional face and body products and while not all the ingredients are bad for you, some are.

The best way to avoid unhealthy chemicals in your products is to read and to learn to understand what is on the label. The most harmful ingredients tend to be those that are added to make a product last longer—for example, preservatives; or to make it feel nicer on the skin, such as mineral oils and silicones; or give it a "signature" scent, like perfumes. These ingredients give no actual benefit to your skin and can be quite toxic.

Product	Ingredient	What to look for	Worrying effects
Antibacterial facewash	Bacteriocides	Triclosan, Benzalkonium chloride, Chlorohexidine	Skin irritation, promotes bacterial resistance. Also found in toothpaste and mouthwash.
Deodorants	Aluminum	Aluminum chlorohydrate, Aluminum zirconium	Neurotoxin linked to Alzheimer's disease. May also contribute to heart and lung disease and fertility problems. Also found in make-up products.
Face & body lotions	Mineral oils	Parafinnum liquidum, Petrolatum	Skin irritants, allergens, potential carcinogens. Also found in baby oils and lipsticks.
	Silicones	Cyclomethicone, Dimethicone, Simethicone, Cyclopentasiloxane, Dimethicone	Skin irritation, blocked pores. Some silicones are tumor promoters and accumulate in liver and lymph nodes. Non-biodegradable. Also found in hair conditioners and most make-up.
	Preservatives	Parabens (methylparaben, ethylparaben, butylparaben, propylparaben, etc.), EDTA, Formaldehyde, Quaternium 15, Methylisothiazolinone	Skin irritation and allergic reactions. Can be neurotoxic. Some, like parabens, are suspected hormone disrupters. Also found in all cosmetics and toiletries.

Some, like harsh detergents and antibacterial agents, are just plain unnecessary—you can get the job done with much milder ingredients and better attention to hygiene.

When you buy toiletries and cosmetics, buy organic products that are free from synthetic preservatives, fragrances, colors, and so on. Use this table to help you identify those ingredients it would be wise to avoid.

Product	Ingredient	What to look for	Worrying effects
Hairspray	Phthalates	Dibutyl phthalate (DBP), Diethylhexyl phthalate (DEHP)	Hormone-disrupting plasticizers that "fix" the fragrance onto the skin. Can cause damage to liver, lungs, and kidneys. May affect fertility and fetal development. Also found in nail polish and perfumed products.
Perfumed products	Fragrances	Parfum	Parfum is a mixture of dozens of synthetic chemicals that are linked to asthma, skin irritation, nausea, mood changes, depression, lethargy, irritability, and memory lapses.
Shampoo & bodywash	Detergents	Sodium lauryl sulfate, Cocamidopropyl betaine, Ammonium lauryl sulfate, Cocamide DEA, Cocamide MEA	Skin irritation. Can promote the formation of cancer-causing substances known as nitrosamines in products during storage. Also found in bubble bath and liquid hand soaps.
Suncare products	Sunscreens	Benzophenone-3, Homosalate, 4-methyl-benzylidene camphor (4-MBC), Octyl-methoxycinnamate, Octyl-dimethyl-PABA, Octocrylene	Hormone-disrupting chemicals known to affect the fertility of animals in the wild. Also found in moisturizers, lipsticks, and foundations.

CAMPAIGN!

We can all do things in our everyday lives that help to change the world for the better. But the biggest changes happen when other people come on board too—particularly those who make policy decisions.

Campaigning tools

Choose a method that suits your cause and your audience.

Letters and emails to decisionmakers, opinion formers, or local newspapers explain and argue the case for your cause.

Petitions raise and demonstrate support.

Leaflets help to present information about your campaign in a simple and accessible way.

Demonstrations can be a great way to get publicity, as long as they are perceived positively.

Direct action, such as boycotting goods, has a direct impact on the situation, as well as getting publicity.

The media—newspapers, radio, and television—can be used to reach a large audience and publicize an event, raise support, or share news of your successes.

A good campaign needs planning. You should think carefully about what you want to achieve, how you are going to do it and how long it should take.

Figure out your goals

You need to figure out exactly what you are trying to achieve—and be able to explain it simply—so that:

- Other people can sign up to your campaign
- Your energy is focused
- You can figure out what you need to do
- You know when you've done it!

Make a strong case

To have an impact on the people you want to influence, you must demonstrate why your issue matters to them. You will need to gather evidence and get as much accurate information as possible to support your case.

How to achieve your aims

Working together The greatest resource of a campaign is the number of people prepared to take part.

- You will probably need to build a team of people to help.
- You should also build partnerships with other groups, local organizations, local businesses, supporters, and so on.
- Ensure that everyone involved is giving the same message.

Learn how decisions are made Find out who makes the decisions, and who influences them. Local politicians will study local newspapers. Businesses listen to their customers.

Find out when decisions are made For instance, when are your local elections or key company meetings?

Feeling overwhelmed?

Some problems may seem too huge for you to make any impact, but every problem has a local angle. If you are concerned about climate change, for example, you could start by looking at how much carbon dioxide your household, company, or city produces—then challenge people to do something about it.

Get your message across

Depending on your issue, you might need to reach decisionmakers, influencers, and supporters.

They could include:

- Your state or local government
- Federal government
- Trade unions
- Local businesses
- Global corporations
- Campaign groups
- The media
- Your local community
- Local schools
- Local celebrities

How to write a campaign letter

- Try to find the name of a relevant, influential person.
- Introduce yourself.
- Make your message brief, with a positive solution.
- Include some brief facts and background information.
- Always ask for an answer.
- Keep it short. If more information is needed, add background notes, such as references to relevant magazine articles, and so on.
- File it. Keep copies of letters and responses.

MAKE FRUIT & FLOWER CORDIALS

Why not make cordials with berries and flowers so that you can enjoy the deliciously light taste of summer long after the season is over? Made and stored properly, these concentrated syrups should last several months, and will make great presents.

There is nothing quite as refreshing as the delicately scented taste of an elder cordial, particularly if it is homemade using hand-picked elder flowers. Clusters of the small white or cream flowers appear in late spring; use freshly-picked flowers for the best taste. Or gather fresh berries and make all sorts of alternative flavors.

Cordials make delicious pure fruit drinks when added to non-carbonated or carbonated water or lemonade, or try mixing elder flower cordial with white wine and carbonated water for a sensationally different spritzer. The concentrated syrups can also be used to enhance desserts or make sorbets and mousses.

Basic cordial recipe

(makes 1¾ pints/ 1 liter)

Ingredients

15 large heads of elder flowers, or 1 lb 1 oz (500 g) fresh fruit, such as strawberries, raspberries, blackberries, or blueberries
2 cups (500 ml) water
1 lemon
2 lb (900 g) caster sugar
3 tbsp (40 g) tartaric/citric acid

Method

■ If using berries, crush them slightly first, as this helps to release the flavors.
■ In a clean pan, bring the water to the boil.
■ Meanwhile, slice the lemon thinly and place in a large glass bowl along with the elder flower heads or berries, sugar, and tartaric/citric acid.
■ As soon as the water has boiled, pour it into the bowl and stir until all the sugar has dissolved.
■ Leave the bowl to cool, then cover and place somewhere cool and dark for four days.
■ Using a clean spoon, taste the concentrate to see if it is strong enough. If it requires further steeping, leave it in the fridge for another day or so.
■ Strain through a sieve lined with cheese cloth.
■ Decant into sterilized bottles. Keeps in the fridge for up to six months.

USE NATURAL CLEANERS & POLISHES

As we scrub and polish to keep dirt and germs at bay, many of the products we use are actually more risky than the germs and dirt themselves. Use environmentally-friendly cleaners instead.

It is ironic that while most modern cleaning products remove surface dirt and sometimes germs, they also make the air and surfaces dirty with industrial chemicals, hydrocarbons, chlorine, and more. But what could green cleaning possibly have to offer that would compete with today's modern formulations?

■ **A cleaner home** Instead of washing away dirt with synthetic chemicals, or masking unpleasant smells with heavy perfumes (which can trigger asthma and headaches), you'll be getting your home really clean.

■ **It costs less** Using readily available ingredients, such as vinegar, means that you will spend less money on cleaners.

■ **Nothing dangerous under the sink** A much safer way to live, especially if you have children. You can clean most floors with hot water and a tiny amount of eco-friendly dishwashing liquid, giving them a good rinse afterward, or try making your own floor cleaner *(right)*.

Wooden floor polishes

Wood flooring is the epitome of unadulterated naturalness. Compared to carpeting, wood is a cleaner flooring that helps keep levels of allergenic dust mites down and requires fewer cleaners to keep it looking good. It doesn't need "nourishing" or "feeding;"

Floor cleaner recipe

In a bucket of water mix together:

¼ cup liquid soap

½–1 cup distilled vinegar or lemon juice

To enhance the fragrance, you can add 1 cup of strong, freshly brewed herb tea of your choice.

instead, an occasional polish keeps the wood looking nice and prevents it from losing moisture. However, most commercial wood floor polishes contain flammable and neurotoxic ingredients. The health problems most often associated with polishes—everything from headaches to depression and asthma—are due to the inhalation of fumes or vapors.

Unvarnished wood can be cleaned and polished easily and beautifully with very simple compounds. A dab of vinegar on a slightly damp cloth is an effective cleaner, while a little light olive oil on a cloth will polish and protect your wood. Or make your own beeswax polish *(below)*. Apply it sparingly with a lint-free cloth (microfiber cloths are ideal) and buff well.

Make your own wooden floor polish

Grate ¼ cup beeswax into a small ceramic bowl or glass-measuring cup (grating helps to speed up the melting process). Put the bowl into a shallow pan of boiling water.

When the beeswax has completely melted, remove it from the heat and slowly add ¼ cup of turpentine. Mix thoroughly. Turpentine, made from the resin of coniferous trees, is an environmentally-friendly solvent.

Transfer the mixture to a small, clean, screw-top jar or pot. Terpentine can have a strong odor, so add a few drops of lavender, orange, lemon, pine oil, or other aromatic essential oil extract to the mix when the polish is cool, but still soft.

GIVE ECO PRESENTS

When it comes to buying presents, we may not always be as ecologically minded as we are with other purchases, but an original, thoughtfully chosen present that makes a positive difference to the environment can be just as pleasurable to give.

1 **Tree—a gift for life** Dedicate a tree in someone's honor, or give a "Grow-a-tree" kit.

2 **Solar-powered gadget** Use the sun's free, renewable, and endless supply of energy to power an iPod or charge a cell phone. Good for people who are always on the go.

3 **Homemade jams & pies** Choose your favorite recipe and get to work in the kitchen. The best part is designing your own labels.

4 **Water barrel** Collects and stores rainwater for watering the garden. Reduces water consumption, as well as water bills.

5 **Vegetable & fruit box scheme** Kick-start a food revolution by giving a trial month's worth of local, organic food grown by small, local producers. It's healthy, delicious, and good for the environment.

6 **Organic linens** Soft, cosy, and luxurious, organic bed sheets, comforters, and pillowcases are made from raw materials produced without harsh chemical treatments.

7 **Bicycle** Harness a loved one's pedal power with a new, upgraded, or secondhand bike.

8 **Wooden toys for children** Plastics are used in 80 percent of new toys; eschew plastic toys and choose natural wood next time you shop for children's toys.

9 **"No sweat" sneakers** Fashionable sneakers and athletic shoes made by fair-trade labor and using rubber soles from sustainably managed forests

10 **Foraged produce** It takes time and effort to forage for edibles, which will surely be appreciated by the recipient of a jar full of chestnuts or some wild blackberries.

⑪ Recycled glass homeware Stylish and ethical wine glasses, pitchers, and decanters made from recycled glass are the height of eco design.

⑫ Membership to an environmental organization There are many worthwhile groups promoting a more sustainable way of life.

⑬ Charitable gift From tree seedlings to health & hygiene kits, a donation to a charity will help provide basic necessities to those who need it in the developing world—and is a perfect gift for someone who has everything.

⑭ Homemade liqueur Take a bottle of gin, vodka, or whiskey and add your choice of fruit; sloe gin or raspberry vodka make wonderfully delicious gifts.

⑮ Organic bodycare products The skin absorbs most of what we put on it, so opt for organic essential oils, herbs, and other natural ingredients when giving a pampering bodycare present.

⑯ A cloth diaper set Easy to use, and better for a baby and the environment; help a new parent make a dent in the tons of diaper waste going to landfill with a set of reusables.

⑰ "Time" gift certificates Anything from gardening help, childcare, or a candlelit meal, a gift of your time can be tailored specifically to the recipient.

⑱ Reusable shopping bag Help someone get over a plastic bag addiction with a handy, long-lasting shopping bag made from cotton, linen, or hemp.

⑲ Books promoting sustainable activities These could include guides for bicycling, walking, camping, or any and all types of flora and fauna.

WEAR & SLEEP IN NATURAL ORGANIC FABRICS

Why wear natural organic fabrics like cotton, wool, linen, and hemp? Natural fibers allow the skin to breathe more easily than most synthetic fibers, and have a less harmful impact on the environment.

We all wear and decorate our homes with many different fabrics. As well as looking good, fabrics have to be soft against the skin, robust enough to be tugged or sat on, warm, waterproof, washable, crease-resistant, or just plain comfy. With all these demands, it is little wonder that we rarely stop to think about what our clothes are actually made of and how textiles might be affecting our health or the environment.

The pyjamas and bedsheets you sleep in probably spend more time in contact with your skin than anything in your wardrobe. As you sweat at night, your skin becomes moist, allowing some of the chemicals that may be on a fabric to be more easily absorbed by your skin. So you may want to think most about these fabrics.

Four good things about natural fibers

■ Natural fibers wick water and sweat away from the skin, so they are more breathable than synthetic fibers.

■ Natural fabrics are usually easier to dye than synthetic ones, so fewer chemicals are needed to manufacture them.

■ Natural fibers will rot away. You can even put discarded clothes on a compost heap.

■ Natural fibers are made from renewable resources that can be regrown. Synthetics are made from oil, which cannot be replaced once it has been used.

Buy organic fabrics

Don't just assume that if your textiles are natural, they are good for the environment. Even natural textiles, or rather the way they are grown, can be extremely damaging. Many of these problems are avoided with organically produced fabrics:

■ Cotton is the most heavily sprayed crop on earth. It is responsible for over ten percent of all pesticides sold, causing poisonings, water contamination, and soil damage all around the world.

■ Cotton has been genetically modified to tolerate herbicides or to resist insect pests. In the US, over three quarters of the cotton crop is GM. In theory, cotton engineered to make its own pesticides should need fewer chemical sprays. However, different insect pests are taking over and the main cotton pests are becoming resistant to the GM cotton, meaning that farmers still have to spray their crops just as often.

Natural organic cotton clothes, pyjamas, baby clothes, and towels cause less harm to the environment, and you and your children will be exposed to fewer potentially harmful chemicals from fabric treatments and finishes.

Manufacturing processes

Most fibers go through some chemical processing before being sold as clothing. These include:

● Dyeing and bleaching
Many dyes have been linked to allergies. The worst are those used on synthetic fabrics.

● Chemical treatments
Easy-care fabrics, for example, are treated using a process that releases formaldehyde and ammonia. Treated fabrics can cause contact dermatitis in susceptible people.

● Plasticized printing
Plastic designs printed onto fabric can contain very high levels of phthalates—chemicals that have a hormonal effect and are potentially carcinogenic. Children who chew and suck their clothing may ingest these compounds.

● Insecticides and fungicides
These are sometimes used on fabrics while they are being stored in warehouses.

Shopping tips

You can help to combat many of the worst social, environmental, and health problems caused by the textile industry by shopping wisely:

Buy organic fibers whenever possible.

Buy alternative natural fibers Linen, hemp, wool, and silk are all better for the environment than non-organically produced materials.

Avoid cheap clothing The true cost of a $6 T-shirt is probably abusive labor practices and environmentally harmful production methods.

Buy secondhand clothes in thrift stores.

Look for fleece and other fabrics made from recycled plastics.

Avoid "disposable fashion" Invest in better-made, more durable items of clothing that won't end up in a landfill site after being worn only a few times.

After you've bought new clothes and fabrics, wash them first before using them to rinse out many of the processing and storage chemicals that might otherwise end up in contact with your skin. Avoid dry-cleaning clothes, as the solvents used can damage the environment.

Fiber guide

Natural fibers These fibers come directly from plants or animals. They include wool, cotton, linen, hemp, and silk (from the cocoons of silkmoth caterpillars that feed on mulberry leaves).

Semi-synthetic The raw ingredient for viscose (rayon) and acetate is cellulose, made from wood chips. Cellulose fibers are found in all plants, and make up the bulk of wood. The cellulose is dissolved using chemical processes, then the mixture is squeezed through a spinneret, which has many small holes, to make fine filaments.

Synthetic fibers The raw ingredients for synthetic fibers are produced by the petrochemical industry from crude oil. They include nylon, acrylic, and polyester. The most common type of polyester is also used for packaging, and plastic bottles can be recycled to make clothing. PVC (polyvinyl chloride) is used for many products, including clothing. Making and disposing of PVC creates and releases dioxin, one of the most toxic chemicals there is.

GO GREEN IN THE PLAYROOM

The toys you purchase can have a positive influence, not just on the workers or the environment where the toys are made, but also on the imagination and creativity of your children. It just takes a little thought about where a toy is from, how it was made, what it is made of, and how a child could use it.

Avoid harmful chemicals

Children are particularly vulnerable to the effects of chemical exposure, as they go through so many developmental changes. Young children suck or chew anything within their reach, so it makes sense to avoid toys and equipment that contain harmful chemicals.

■ Buy toys made from natural products such as wood, cotton, hemp, and wool.

■ Choose toys that use non-toxic dyes, paints, and natural oil finishes such as linseed and beeswax.

■ Avoid soft plastic toys. Many contain plasticizers called phthalates that are known to be harmful. These have been banned from toys in many countries, but can still be found in clothing with plastic designs, stroller covers, and so on.

Fair play

Choosing toys that have been made according to ethical standards, such as those of TransFair USA, ensures that workers get fair wages and that there has been no abuse of child labor.

■ Avoid toys produced by global brands unless you are sure of their employment practices.

■ Think local: buy from local craftspeople or community-based toy making groups if possible.

Stay green by reusing toys

One of the greenest things you can do is to avoid buying new toys.

● Exchange toys with friends.

● Use toy-swap schemes.

● Sell and buy used toys at garage sales or on the internet.

● Invent "alternative" toys. A cardboard box and a wooden spoon can provide hours of entertainment for very young children.

● Make your own. For example, try making your own modeling dough using flour and vegetable oil.

You could also:

● Ask toy manufacturers about their employment policies: 75% of all toys are made in China, where millions of workers work long hours for low pay, often in dangerous conditions.

FORAGE FOR FUNGI

If you have ever been lucky enough to pick a basket of field mushrooms and bring them home to eat, you will know that nothing beats the intensity of their flavor and the wonderful aroma that they give off. You too can learn to find and identify the right mushrooms for the most delicious harvest.

It's not usual to be able to pick field mushrooms all year round, but you can forage for a wide variety of fungi for several months—mainly in late summer and fall, and also in spring and even in winter, depending on where you live, for a few species such as winter mushroom (*Flammulina velutipes*). Wild fungi will not grow where chemical fertilizers or sprays have been used, so not only are your pickings free, you can be sure that they are pesticide-free, too.

If you are a beginner, start by joining a guided fungi excursion or a fungi course, or by teaming up with an experienced forager. This will help you to know where to look, to tell the difference between various species, and to recognize what stage of growth the mushrooms are at.

Fungi do not use energy from the sun, as plants do, to make their food. Instead, they absorb food and water from their surroundings. The edible parts are the fruiting bodies, which change in appearance according to the weather and as they mature. They grow in a wide variety of environments, but the best places to look for them are woodlands (especially clearings or the edges of woodlands), old pastures where horses or cattle have grazed, and grassland.

Although correct identification is the first step in safe harvesting, you also need to pay attention to the condition of a mushroom. An overripe or decomposing mushroom can cause digestive upsets, and some people react with skin rashes to certain edible species.

On the menu

There are about 100 mushrooms that are known to be edible. Some of these are so prized—such as the King Bolete and Chanterelle—that seasoned fungi hunters try to keep their locations a secret. Here is a selection of the best varieties.

Parasol
(Lepiota procera)
Scaly brown/gray cap that opens like an umbrella. Remove stem before cooking. Grows in clearings and yards.

Morel
(Morchella esculenta)
Pitted brownish cap. Must be cooked. Appears in spring in woodlands, clearings, and in hedges.

Shaggy mane
(Coprinus comatus)
White, scaly fungus. Gills change from white to pink, brown, then black. Grows in grassy places.

Giant puffball
(Langermannia gigantean)
White, ball-shaped. Pick when young before flesh turns yellow. Grows in meadows, pastures, and under hedges.

Chanterelle
(Cantharellus cibarius)
Yellow wavy-edged cap and stalk. Grows in woodland clearings.

Bay bolete
(Boletus badius)
Pale to chestnut brown cap with yellow pores on the underside. Pick when young. Grows in woods.

King bolete
(Boletus edulis)
Brownish, bun-shaped cap. Bulbous stalk. Check cap for insects before eating. Grows in woodlands and hedges.

Meadow mushroom
(Agaricus campestris)
Whitish cap with pink gills and a thin ring around the stem. Grows in pastures and meadows.

Off the menu

Some mushrooms are poisonous, a few of which are identified below, and the effects can vary from a stomach upset to severe, or even fatal, liver damage. The Shaggy parasol (*Macrolepiota rhacodes*) (*right*) can cause stomach upsets.

**Fly agaric
(*Amanita muscaria*)**
Scarlet with white patches, which fade as it matures.

**Death cap
(*Amanita phalloides*)**
Distinctive white gills with a sheath at the base of the stalk.

**Yellow stainer
(*Agaricus xanthodermus*)**
The white cap turns grayish with age. Flesh is bright yellow.

**Ugly milk cap
(*Lactarius torminosus*)**
Woolly-looking cap that forms a depression in the middle.

Foraging the green way

In some areas fungi are becoming scarce, either as a result of over-gathering or because the habitat where they grow has altered or been destroyed. Try to follow these few simple rules to make sure that more fungi will emerge the following season in the places where you have been foraging.

■ Gather no more than half the fungi present, or a maximum of 3 lb 5 oz (1.5 kg) in weight.

■ Only take as many fungi as you can use.

■ Pick by twisting the stalk, not by cutting, which can damage the network of threads left in the ground.

■ If you are a beginner, go with an experienced forager or take a reliable field guide with you so that you only pick fungi that you can eat.

Foraging tips

● Don't pick on wet days.

● Don't pick decaying fungi.

● Use a basket, not a plastic bag, to bring home your fungi, as they decay quickly in warm, stale air.

● Use mushrooms within 24 hours of picking them.

● Before cooking, cut each fungus in half and throw away any that show signs of maggots, or have white gills.

● Only eat a small amount if the species is new to you in case it disagrees with you.

Mushroom frittata

(serves 2)

This is a simple yet delicious way of cooking wild mushrooms. If you can't go foraging, or wild fungi aren't in season, use chestnut or baby bella mushrooms, which have a good, meaty flavor.

Ingredients

2 tablespoons (25 g) butter
1 cup (85 g) wild, chestnut, or baby bella mushrooms, sliced
1 shallot, finely chopped
1 clove garlic, finely chopped
4 eggs
1 teaspoon fresh thyme, finely chopped
Salt and pepper to taste
A few leaves of fresh basil as a garnish (optional)

Method

■ Melt the butter in a frying pan and cook the mushrooms, shallot, and garlic until they are soft and beginning to take on some color.

■ Beat the eggs with the thyme, salt, and pepper.

■ Pour the egg mixture over the mushrooms and cook gently over a medium heat until set.

■ Slide under the broiler to brown the top, then scatter over the basil leaves if you wish and serve hot or cold.

CHOOSE SAFE PRODUCTS FOR YOUR CHILDREN

You may think of your skin as a barrier, but in reality, it is more like a sponge. It can absorb up to 60 percent of whatever you put on it. Children's skins are particularly vulnerable to the chemicals in bath products and in the environment.

Children differ from adults in a number of ways that can increase their susceptibility to toxins in the home. For example:

■ Children's skin is thinner and more absorbent than that of adults, thus providing a less effective barrier to environmental toxins.

■ Their immune systems are less able to defend against poisons and allergens.

■ They eat, drink, and breathe in more for their weight than adults, and so take in more toxins per pound. Even at rest, an infant will breath in twice the volume of air as an adult.

■ Crawling on the floor and putting objects in their mouths means that young children come into contact with dust and other potentially toxic particles.

Shampoos, body washes, and moisturizers are all easily absorbed through the scalp and skin, so avoid using products that contain synthetic perfumes, colors, and preservatives on your children's skin. You should also avoid using harsh detergents and cleaning products, which can contaminate the air and surfaces in the home.

Checklist for children

Buy fragrance-free, organic bath products (soaps, shampoos, body washes).

Choose plant-based, gentle, organic skincare products (oils, creams, toothpaste).

Treat babies' skins with the utmost care. Buy fragrance- and chemical-free baby wipes, diaper cream, and washable or biodegradable diapers.

Read and understand the label. Avoid cleaning products (disinfectants, bleaches, aerosols, carpet cleaners) that contain harmful chemicals.

A dry skin solution

Using harsh toiletries on sensitive skin may be a contributing factor to the rising rate of eczema and allergies among children. Although parents whose children have skin rashes often approach the problem by applying more products to the skin, cutting out baby toiletries altogether could be a more effective solution.

If your child has dry or irritated skin, try making your own herbal wash bag.

Cut the foot off an old pair of tights, about 6 in (15 cm) from the end, for a pouch.

Fill the pouch with a handful of oatmeal and, if you wish, some soothing herbs such as chamomile or lavender.

Tie a knot in the open end of the pouch.

Use in the bathtub or shower. One wash bag will last one day maximum—keep it in the fridge in a plastic bag if you intend to use it morning and night, but don't try to store it for longer, as it can accumulate bacteria. When wet, it will produce a lovely, creamy liquid that will clean and nourish skin without drying it. Great for babies and children, but also good for adults.

2 ROOF TERRACE, PATIO, OR TINY YARD

GROW BEANS ON A TEEPEE

If you want to grow vegetables that will give you a crop over many weeks and also make an attractive, leafy screen on your patio or balcony, plant some pole beans. They don't take up much ground space, and the more you pick the tender, crunchy beans, the more the plants produce. The flowers on bean plants are so striking—scarlet, white, pink, or bicolored—that garden designers often include them in their designs.

Beans need to grow in well-fertilized soil that is rich in compost. Runner beans *(Phaseolus coccineus)* and the finer green beans *(Phaseolus vulgaris)*, also called string or snap beans, will need some kind of support to help them climb, and teepees are the best—and prettiest—option. If you don't have space for a teepee, grow a dwarf type of bean that doesn't need support, such as runner beans "Pickwick" and "Hestia," or string beans such as "Annabel."

Growing beans from seed

Both kinds of bean need a sheltered, sunny spot. The soil needs to be a minimum temperature of 50°F (10°C) for the seeds to germinate.

The seeds will get off to a quicker start if you sow them indoors, one seed per pot, at a depth of 1½ in (4 cm).

Water the pots well, put on a sunny window sill and don't let the soil dry out.

If you are sowing outdoors, it's best to warm the soil first for green beans by covering it with black plastic for a couple of weeks before sowing. Seedlings sown indoors should be ready to plant out in about three weeks, but make sure you put them outside for a few days beforehand to harden them off.

Planting bean seedlings

■ The container you choose should be at least 18 in (45 cm) in diameter, with drainage holes and terracotta at the bottom.

■ Fill the container with a mixture of commercial potting soil, sphagnum moss, and vermiculite.

■ Before planting the seedlings, fix the teepee in place. You can buy a teepee to fit the size of the pot, or make your own using four or five 6 ft (2 m) tall bamboo poles. Push the poles into the ground around the edge of the container until they touch the bottom of the pot. Gather the tops of the poles together and secure them with string to form a teepee shape.

■ Plant out the seedlings, one by each pole. Tie the seedlings onto the poles as they climb. When each plant reaches the top of its support, pinch out the tips of the plant.

■ Keep the containers well watered (green beans can tolerate hotter, drier conditions) and feed the plants with a liquid fertilizer if they need a boost.

■ Start harvesting from midsummer for tender young beans, snipping them off with a pair of scissors. Both runner beans and green beans freeze well if you have a glut.

Grow potatoes in a container

You can also grow a crop of delicious potatoes by planting them in a container or barrel. You can make your own potato-growing containers using a wooden barrel, a deep plastic pot or wooden box at least 12 in (30 cm) in diameter, or even an old (but clean!) garbage can.

■ Make sure that your container is positioned in a light spot, and has drainage holes and a layer of terracotta at the bottom.

■ Use well-sprouted seed potatoes and choose fast-growing early varieties (planted in early spring) and second earlies (about a month later).

■ Fill the container with a 4–5 in (10–12.5 cm) layer of good potting soil and stand the potatoes on top of the soil, with the sprouts facing upward and positioned about 7 in (18 cm) apart. A pot that is 12–16 in (30–40 cm) in diameter and about 16 in (40 cm) deep will accommodate a maximum of two seed potatoes.

■ Water the soil well, and when the potato shoots are about 6 in (15 cm) tall, cover them with another layer of compost so that the tips of the plants are just showing. Continue to build up the soil in this way until the shoots are just below the rim of the container.

■ Keep the container well watered, especially if the weather is hot. Once the pretty flowers have appeared, feed weekly with a liquid organic feed.

■ In early summer, check on the size of the potatoes by scraping away some of the soil around them.

■ Once the potatoes are about the size of an egg, you can dig them out and prepare a dish of your own nutritious and tasty homegrown new potatoes.

KEEP URBAN HONEY BEES

Bees are an important part of an organic ecosystem, but you don't need to own a rural retreat in order to keep bees and harvest their honey: a small yard, or even a rooftop terrace, is a perfect place for a beehive—all you need is a flat outdoor space.

Urban beekeepers have the advantage that cities tend to be warmer than rural areas, so the bees are more active and their season for foraging for nectar is longer. And with a far greater selection of plants on display in highly planted parks, gardens, and window boxes, there's often something in flower all year round (depending, of course, on the local climate). This means that urban bees have the potential to produce a richer variety of honey and higher yields.

Bees prefer to have a clear flight path upward out of the hive, which should face south if possible. From an urban beekeeper's point of view, it's also worth keeping the hive in a secluded place to avoid people being stung. If you have a yard without any high walls, plant tall shrubs or hedges or erect a fence to encourage the bees' flight path up and over peoples' heads. Once they are up in the air, the bees go in various directions to forage.

Getting started

There are many beekeeping societies and groups who will be happy to help in providing advice, equipment, and the bees to get you started.

Beneficial properties of honey

- Honey contains vitamins and antioxidants, and enzymes that help in its digestion.
- It's an excellent natural preservative.
- Honey has been used in healing remedies for at least 4,000 years. It is now known to act as an antiseptic/antibacterial agent, and is most commonly used as an anti-microbial agent used for dressing wounds, burns, and skin ulcers.

PLANT BLUEBERRY BUSHES

There are many good reasons for growing your own blueberries: they are delicious to eat, either fresh or in pies; they are a "superfood" containing high levels of antioxidants that have anti-ageing benefits, help to keep your eyes healthy and can protect against cancer; and they make delightful garden plants, with scented flowers in spring, dusty-blue fruits and brilliant foliage in the fall. Once you get a taste for blueberries, you'll want to eat a handful every day; picking your own bush-ripened berries means they'll always be at their freshest.

Until recently, it was thought that blueberries could only be grown in large beds of acidic soil. Now we know that they can thrive in containers, given the right conditions, and that the soil in these pots doesn't have to be 100 percent acid potting soil. In fact, specialist growers are now recommending that the soil for blueberries in containers consists of at least 50 percent fine-composted pine or fir bark. Most blueberries need another blueberry plant of a different variety for pollination, so check with your local grower or nursery before buying your plants.

Caring for blueberries in containers

Growing blueberries in containers is a great way of producing a crop of delicious fruit in a small space. However, plants in pots are more susceptible to cold winter temperatures than those grown in open ground, and you will need to protect them from freezing conditions.

The roots of blueberries are less cold hardy than the shoots, and plant damage can occur when the soil temperature falls below 32°F. The easiest way to prevent this is to bring your pots into an unheated shed, root cellar, or garage, but remember that the plants will still need some light, and you should also water them from time to time.

In the summer, containers dry out quickly and will need frequent watering. Make sure that you soak the whole root ball each time you water, to prevent the roots from growing up to the surface of the pot (where they will be even more prone to drying out) to search for moisture. It is equally important not to let the plant sit in water.

Blueberries in pots need

■ A free-draining acidic soil.

■ Moisture throughout the growing season, although the pots should not be waterlogged.

■ A top dressing in spring with a slow-release fertilizer.

■ Pruning in winter: cut out any weak or damaged stems and, once the bush is three years old, cut one or two of the oldest stems down to ground level to encourage new shoots to grow.

■ Pick the fruit when they are fully blue and ripe.

For successful crops

■ Make sure that the composted bark you use is untreated.

■ Take off all but about five or six flowers in the first year of growth so that the plants become well established before they put their energy into fruiting.

■ Use rainwater if possible, although tap water is better than not watering at all.

■ Don't use animal manure or animal-based fertilizers, or tomato fertilizer.

Good blueberry varieties to grow

Northern highbush (varieties of *Vaccinium corymbosum*) can grow to 6 ft (2 m) tall in the ground, but will be more compact in containers.

"Duke" grows to about 1.5 m (5 ft) and crops in mid-summer.

"Bluecrop" produces good crops of large berries in late summer.

"Herbert" is one of the best varieties for flavor, and has bright red foliage in the fall. Fruits ripen in late summer.

Half-high blueberries (hybrids between *Vaccinium angustifolium* and *V corymbosum*) are hardy and more compact, growing to about 5 ft (1.5 m).

"Northblue" produces its large berries in early summer.

Most southern highbush blueberries (complex hybrids) are evergreen and cannot survive very cold winter temperatures.

"Sunshine Blue" is compact, has an excellent flavor and can tolerate less acidic soils.

Blueberry muffins

Ingredients

1¼ cups wholewheat all-purpose flour

1¼ cups all-purpose flour

2 teaspoons baking powder

1 teaspoon baking soda

¼ cup butter

¼ cup honey

1 cup fresh or ⅔ cup dried blueberries

1 egg, lightly beaten

1¼ cup natural yogurt

Method

■ Preheat the oven to 180°C/350°F.

■ Mix the flours, baking powder, and soda together in a bowl. Make a well in the center.

■ Gently melt the butter and honey in a pan, pour into the well with the blueberries, egg, and yogurt and very gently mix into the flour, allowing the mixture to remain slightly lumpy. Don't over-mix or the muffins will be heavy.

■ Spoon the mixture into muffin tins lined with muffin cases. Bake for 20 minutes or until the tops are light brown.

Variation
Cranberry & orange muffins

Replace the blueberries with ⅔ cup dried cranberries and the grated zest of 2 oranges.

GROW AN APPLE TREE IN A POT

You don't have to own acres of land to grow your own apples. All you need is the right kind of apple tree, potting soil, and a pot. Then, as long as you remember to water and feed it, you should get showers of pretty blossoms in spring, followed by your own crop of juicy apples in the fall.

Buying the right kind of apple is important, so it's a good idea to get help from a fruit tree nursery. Apples are grown on a range of different rootstocks (the plant that provides the root system), depending on the size and form of the tree required. For pot-grown apples, the best rootstock is M.26, which will produce dwarf trees either as bushes, single-stemmed trees grown at an oblique angle, or single-stemmed, column-shaped trees. Decide what shape you want, and whether you want more than one tree. If you only have room for one, choose a self-pollinating apple such as Jonathan, Golden Delicious, or Yellow Transplant. If you buy two or more apple trees, make sure they are from the same pollination group, and look for disease-resistant varieties that crop well. Your supplier should be able to advise you.

Three easy steps

■ Plant a one-year-old tree in late fall in a pot about 12–15 in (30–38 cm) in diameter. Put a layer of broken clay pots at the bottom for drainage and fill with equal parts compost, vermiculite, and peat moss. Place in a sheltered spot out of the prevailing wind. Increase the watering in the spring and give it liquid fertilizer.

■ Prune your tree to shape it and make a good framework of branches that will bear plenty of fruit. Ask for pruning instructions when you buy the plant.

■ Transplant your tree into a larger pot every year until it is fully grown. After that, prune the roots every three years or so and refill the pot with fresh soil.

Tips on growing an apple tree

Stand the pot on bricks to help with drainage.

In the winter, water sparingly, making sure that the soil does not dry out completely. Move the pot to a sheltered spot out of the prevailing wind. If a heavy frost is expected, wrap the pot in burlap.

In the spring, increase watering and start feeding with a liquid fertilizer recommended by your local nursery.

In midsummer the pot may need watering twice a day. Feed every 7–10 days.

You can grow other fruits in pots—pears, peaches, nectarines, apricots, and figs—but these plants need extra protection and care.

START A WORM COMPOSTER

Nearly 40 percent of our domestic refuse is organic material—things like vegetable and fruit peelings, tea bags, and food scraps—which can and should be recycled. If they're sent to landfill sites, they produce methane, a potent greenhouse gas that contributes to global warming, and a liquid called leachate, which can contaminate water supplies.

An excellent way of being environmentally responsible and recycling your own organic waste is to feed it to a colony of worms in a worm composter. These obliging wrigglers devour the waste (each worm eats up to half its body weight every day) in a dark bin and produce two natural byproducts: a top quality compost that gardeners sometimes call "Black Gold," which you can use to condition the soil in your garden and in containers; and a liquid that you can dilute to make a superb tonic for your plants.

You can make your own worm composter, using stackable storage boxes, wire mesh, a drain cock, and synthetic carpet for a lid, but the simplest way to get started is to buy a readymade kit, complete with a supply of the same kind of worms that normally live in well-rotted manure or compost heaps.

Indoors or outdoors?

Worm composters are often described as "odor free," but many people find that when they lift the lid off to add more scraps, a strong earthy smell wafts out. So, it may be a better idea to keep your worm composter in a utility room or outside the back door, rather than in the kitchen. Even if you like the earthy smell, you may find that the liquid that you need to siphon off too pungent. When draining off this liquid, use rubber gloves and store the concentrated plant food in a jar with a tight lid until you need to use it. Then dilute it 1:10

with water and watch your plants perk up within days. Another reason for keeping the bin outside is that fruit flies are often attracted to the waste in summer and lay their eggs in it. They're harmless, but a nuisance in the kitchen.

What composting worms like

■ A mixture of dry and wet waste, such as vegetable scraps, fruit peelings and cores, egg shells, coffee grains, tea bags, cardboard from egg cartons and toilet rolls, shredded paper, dust from the vacuum cleaner.

■ Dark, moist (but not wet) living conditions, at a fairly constant temperature. Keep them out of scorching heat in the summer, and protected from frost during winter (for example, with an insulation jacket).

■ Good air circulation.

■ Regular amounts of waste, chopped up small or shredded.

What composting worms don't like

■ Too thick a layer of waste above them, which cuts off their air supply and makes their living conditions sour and airless.

■ Too many foods that make the conditions acid, such as onions and lemons.

■ Waterlogged living conditions—the liquid at the bottom needs to be drained off frequently and dry waste, especially cardboard, needs to be added regularly.

How it works

The worm composter is a bin (usually plastic) with a lid, and layers or chambers through which the worms move as they eat up the waste.

There is a collector tray at the bottom that holds the liquid that is produced, with a tap to run it off. The lowest chamber has a layer of bedding where the worms live at first.

As you add small amounts of waste, the worms wriggle up the chambers to eat it—they can eat at least half their own weight in a day—and their casts (droppings) sink down.

Once almost full, take out of the bin the "Black Gold" in the bottom chamber and start again. If you provide the right conditions and regularly siphon off the liquid, the worms will go on eating and breeding for years on end.

USE ECO-FRIENDLY DIY MATERIALS

Whether you are considering a building project, painting a room, or just adding new furnishings to your home, there are plenty of ways in which you can lower your impact on the environment and minimize your exposure to potentially hazardous substances.

Reusing materials rather than buying new is always the most environmentally responsible option. So-called "environmental" materials are not actually good for the environment; they are just less damaging than non-environmental materials. It's better to reuse salvaged rainforest hardwoods from a demolished building, for example, than to buy new "ethical" wood. And recycled plastics may be an appropriate choice, even if you normally avoid using plastic.

Try some of these ideas to help you feel good about, and not be made sick by, the materials that surround you in your home.

Choose the right materials

Many of the products recommended for home improvement projects contain very unpleasant chemicals. Check the labels for hazard or health warnings before you buy, and try to source safer alternatives. There are a whole range of natural, responsibly sourced choices if you decide to buy new materials.

Avoid if possible

Polyvinyl Chloride (PVC) is widely used as a construction material for products such as cables, pipes, flooring, and paneling. The production and disposal of PVC creates and releases toxic chemicals into the environment.

Medium Density Fiberboard (MDF) contains urea formaldehyde. The dust generated from cutting or sanding MDF is dangerous, and low levels of the chemical can be released throughout the life of the product.

Timber treatments Many timber treatments are toxic to humans, pets, and wildlife.

Fungicides Many wallpaper pastes contain fungicides.

Harmful solvents Paint strippers, paint thinners, varnish removers, and brush cleaners usually contain very strong and potentially harmful solvents.

Formaldehydes Floor sealants can contain formaldehydes and other harmful chemicals.

Aluminum is very energy-intensive to produce. Use alternatives, such as wood for window frames.

Wood materials

Choose wood that is sustainably harvested and, if possible, from a local source to reduce the impact of transportation.

Timber certified by the Forestry Stewardship Council (FSC) guarantees that your wood is from a well-managed forest that meets strict environmental, social, and economic standards.

Many wood treatments are toxic to human beings, pets, and wildlife. Ask suppliers what has been used to treat the wood before you buy it.

Plywood, chipboard, and MDF tend to be made of waste wood, but the adhesives used to glue the particles together can contain formaldehyde and other unpleasant chemicals.

Consider using recycled plastic "wood" for floors, fences, play equipment, and decks. It prevents plastic drink bottles from going into landfills and can even be recycled again.

VOCs in paints

A major hazard in paints and varnishes is VOCs—Volatile Organic Compounds. In this case the word "organic" is used in the chemical sense, meaning that the compounds contain carbon. "Volatile" means that they evaporate readily at typical room temperatures. If the chemicals are also harmful, it means that they have a high potential for causing health problems because they can easily enter the body. Most paints now carry VOC ratings. Also, not all VOCs are harmful or synthetic. Alcohol and citrus oils are classed as VOCs.

Paints & finishes

Ordinary paints are manufactured from complex synthetic chemicals, some of which can be damaging to health. Natural paints are made using ingredients close to their natural state.

Headaches and allergies are common side effects of decorating and, according to the World Health Organization, professional painters and decorators face a 40 percent higher than average risk of lung cancer. Paint manufacture is also harmful to the environment. Making one ton of ordinary paint results in 10 tons of waste, much of it toxic. Petrochemical solvent-based ("oil-based") paints are recognized as

Make milk paint

Mix ½ lb (250 g) casein powder with 12 fl oz (340 ml) water. Whisk until thick. Stand for 30 minutes.

Add another 4 fl oz (125 ml) of water. Whisk to a creamy consistency. Leave to stand for 15 minutes more.

Mix 2 oz (50 g) of pigment powder with a little water to make a thin paste. Add the casein mix, stir, and use.

being harmful, so many paint manufacturers have developed water-based alternatives. Although lower in smelly solvents (VOCs), water-based paints can contain even more harmful chemicals, and require complex and energy-intensive manufacturing processes.

Choose natural paints

■ The components in natural paint are based on plant oils and extracts such as linseed oil, citrus oils, balsamic turpentine, and simple minerals. They involve less intensive processing, which uses less energy and produces less waste.

■ Natural paints can also be better for your home surfaces. They are slightly porous, so they tend to allow surfaces to "breathe"—unlike most conventional paints, which tend to seal surfaces.

■ Natural paints may cost more than mass-produced petrochemical alternatives, but the hidden costs to your health will be much less.

■ Many natural paints and finishes are widely available. Larger hardware stores often sell natural products and many companies sell via the internet or by mail order.

■ Alternatively, make your own paint. Casein powder, a by-product of milk, can be mixed with water and a small amount of pigment to make a smooth, matte "milk paint" for interior walls.

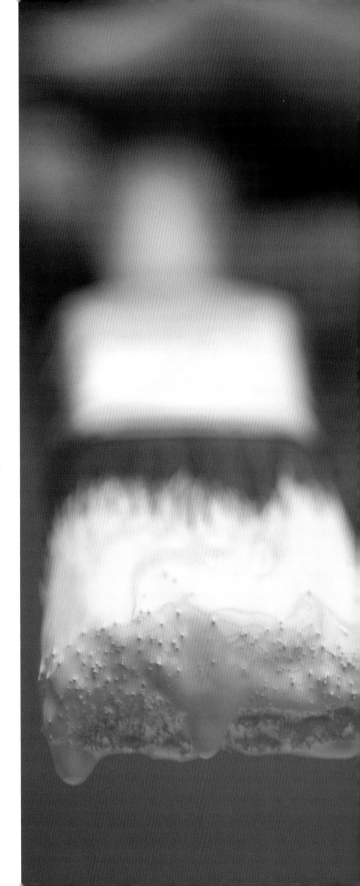

Floorings

Cover your floors with material that is attractive, practical, durable, and environmentally sound: most carpets contain synthetic dyes and a heavy mix of chemicals, so choose natural alternatives instead.

Wool is one of the best materials for carpets. It is hard-wearing and naturally flame-resistant. Although wool carpets tend to be more expensive, if properly cared for, they can last for 50 years or more. Use cork or wool for the underlay. Recycled underlays made from old car tires, fiber scraps, or compressed wood fibers are also available.

Grass rugs or carpets made of sisal, coir, or seagrass are another natural flooring alternative.

Solid timber flooring is a good, natural choice, but check that the wood is sustainably harvested and locally sourced if possible.

Existing wooden floors can often be sanded and used again. If not, consider using reclaimed floorboards.

Floor tiles can be made out of natural materials such as clay or stone. However, you should consider the extraction and transportation implications.

Cork flooring is sourced from the bark of cork oak trees. Mediterranean cork oak forests are harvested sustainably. These forests need all the help they can get—they are less profitable now that many wines are sold with plastic corks.

Natural linoleum (not its PVC imitation) is made from linseed oil and other natural ingredients.

Planning a building project?

Does it need to be done, and do you need to do as much as you think? Major projects involve a lot of work, create a large amount of waste, and require many new materials.

Plan around what is available by designing around fittings and other items that you can salvage. For example, rather than rip out a whole kitchen, just change the cupboard doors to update the look.

Plan for recycling By using nails and screws rather than glue, items will be easier to dismantle in the future and so be more easily reused or recycled.

Try to reuse old bricks.

Assess quantities of paint and other materials to avoid waste.

Think long-term Cheap materials and poor workmanship are likely to need replacing or redoing in a year or two's time, creating more waste. If you budget for the likely cost over decades, rather than the immediate cost of a job, materials that seem expensive may actually save you money.

Extraction and transportation of stone and aggregates can cause environmental problems. Ask your supplier where products have been quarried or obtained.

Cement production is an energy-intensive industry producing vast quantities of carbon dioxide. In fact, cement manufacturing is the third largest cause of manmade carbon dioxide emissions. Try to limit its use where possible.

Using contractors? Look for websites listing environmentally aware contractors and architects.

Decorating a child's bedroom?

Create safe, healthy surroundings that don't cost the earth.

- Use natural paints.
- Use natural flooring materials.
- Avoid wall-to-wall carpets that can house dust mites.
- If you are stripping very old paint, check for lead content. Avoid plastics and PVC; use untreated wood and natural fabrics on cots and other nursery furniture.
- If you are pregnant, be especially careful to avoid potentially toxic ingredients (for example, MDF, which contains formaldehyde). If a label says "danger," "warning," or "caution," ask the retailer for the product's safety data sheet. This will explain the specific hazards involved and how to deal with them. Some ingredients, such as strong acids or strong alkalis, may burn or blind if splashed onto the skin or eyes, but they have no long-term effects on the unborn child.

TRAIN A FIG TREE AGAINST A WALL

It's no wonder figs were a staple food in Ancient Greece and Rome. They thrive in warm, sunny climates where they produce fruit two or three times a year; they are sweet and succulent; and they are packed full of easily digested nutrients. Because they are soft-skinned, they do not travel well and so are best eaten, fully ripe, straight from the tree.

If you have a warm, sheltered wall facing south or southwest, you can grow figs outdoors in a temperate climate. Under glass, with a minimum temperature of 55°F (13°C) from January onward, you should be able to get two crops; outdoors, only one will ripen, even though the tree may form a second crop.

How to grow figs

The best way to grow a fig against a wall is to train it in a fan shape. This provides a lovely covering of big leaves, but for edible fruit, you must give the plant special attention.

■ Restrict the roots to keep the tree compact and make it bear fruit—if you don't, the strong roots will spread through the soil and all you'll get is leaves. You can do this in two ways: by planting the tree in a pot that has good drainage and is at least 18 in (45 cm) in diameter, and sinking it into the ground; or by making a "box" or pit at least 24 in (60 cm) deep, lined with concrete or overlapping sidewalk slabs and with a thick layer of bricks or rubble in the bottom. Both pot and box should be filled with soil-based compost, with pieces of brick or large grit added.

■ Attach vine eyes 8 in (20 cm) apart, starting at 14 in (35 cm) from the ground, up the wall, and fix horizontal wires to them. Keep wires 2–4 in (5–10 cm) away from the wall to allow for air circulation when the plant is tied onto them.

■ Plant the tree 8 in (20 cm) away from the wall. As the tree grows, tie the side shoots to the wires to form a fan shape.

■ Water the tree frequently in the summer, daily if it's very dry, or the developing fruit will drop off.

■ The tiny fruits that form toward the end of the summer need to be protected in winter in cold areas. Cover them with burlap or straw held in place by mesh netting.

■ The fig should be pruned in early spring, and any large fruits on the branches taken off.

What to plant

There are many varieties of fig, some with brown or purple skin and reddish flesh, others with yellowish-green skin and pale flesh.

Brown Turkey The best cropper—does well in Southern California.

Osborn's Prolific very sweet, best fresh. Grows in shade. Good for Pacific Northwest.

Verte A small tree. Fruit is excellent fresh or dried. Recommended for short-summer climates.

You can expect some fruit the first year after planting. Once the tree is carrying a heavy crop, feed with a liquid fertilizer until the figs ripen.

MAKE YOUR OWN BARBECUE

Treat yourself to a green barbecue of delicious foods. Recycle a spare terracotta pot from the garden instead of buying an expensive high-tech metal barbecue, and use charcoal from sustainably managed woodlands.

More than 90 percent of our barbecue charcoal is imported, and much of it is likely to come from unsustainably managed tropical forests. By buying charcoal made from trees that have been coppiced (when trees and shrubs are trimmed back to produce a supply of thin poles) and thinned in woodlands, you are using sustainably produced fuel. Even better, if the charcoal is from a local producer, the carbon dioxide emissions generated by transporting it from the producer to the store can be reduced by as much as 85 percent compared with imported charcoal. As coppicing creates the right conditions for many plants that provide food for butterflies to flourish, you will be helping to conserve threatened species too. So look for charcoal bags that say "locally produced" or "home grown."

Barbecuing using an empty clay pot couldn't be easier. You'll need a pot about 13 in (33 cm) in diameter to feed up to three people, a larger one for more people.

■ Stand the pot on a couple of bricks to allow air to circulate underneath the fire. Fill the pot half full with pebbles or broken clay pots, slightly more if it is tall.

■ Line the top part with tinfoil and heap the charcoal in the center. Use a proprietary barbecue lighter to light the coals.

■ When the coals are glowing red and have started to turn gray at the edges, spread them out evenly and balance an oven shelf or grill pan shelf over the rim of the pot.

■ Cook skewers of peppers, zucchini, and mushrooms, or pieces of fish or meat, and throw a handful of rosemary, thyme, or lavender on the fire for a hint of herby flavor as the skewers are cooking.

PLANT A TREE OR CLIMBER FOR WILDLIFE

Yards, no matter how small, have become incredibly important havens for wildlife. This is because wild creatures have lost many of their feeding and breeding sites in the countryside—either as a result of intensive farming, which makes widespread use of pesticides, or changes in land use. Some creatures, such as moths and bumblebees, are increasingly reliant on our yards for their survival.

If all you have in your yard are a few containers with a selection of flowering plants, you will still have some wildlife: small soil creatures, visiting butterflies, and hoverflies, perhaps, and, if you leave the seedheads on your plants, some seed-eating birds. You'll attract more creatures if your patch has some water, a shrub or two, and a thick climber. But you can offer first-class living quarters to a host of wildlife if you have a small tree.

A tree can provide

■ Plenty of leaves and nectar-rich flowers for insects and their larvae to feed on.

■ Bark for insects to live in and for lichens and mosses with their attendant creatures.

■ Berries and seeds for birds.

■ A layer of leaves at the base of the tree that, if left to decay, creates food and shelter for worms, slugs, snails, pill bugs, and millipedes, which in turn provides food for centipedes, spiders, and beetles.

■ Dead and decaying wood, which provides foods and nesting sites for creatures such as beetles or solitary bees. Eventually, holes in the trunk can create nesting sites for birds.

In a small yard, a tree will probably become the dominant feature, and if you choose a deciduous tree, it will help to bring seasonal changes: new buds, followed by blossoms in the spring; a lush green canopy of leaves in the summer; yellow, orange, or red foliage, plus berries or seeds, in the fall; and a striking silhouette of branches to admire in the winter.

Helping wildlife

● If you have only a roof terrace or balcony and no room for trees or climbers, grow a mixture of flowering plants (with single flowers rather than double) to provide a source of nectar for insects such as butterflies, moths, and bees. You could also fill a shallow dish with water to make a bird bath, attach a lightweight bird feeder to a window, or fix a nesting box to a wall at least six feet off the ground.

● Researchers have found that, as far as insects and invertebrates are concerned, small yards are just as good for wildlife as larger ones. In a survey of biodiversity in 61 private yards ranging in size from 344–10,000 sq ft (32–940 sq m) in the city of Sheffield in the UK, the researchers caught and counted an astonishing 40,000 individual invertebrates, and found nationally rare beetles, bugs, snails, and flies, and a spider that had only previously been recorded on a mountain top.

● Yards make a vital network of wildlife habitats in major cities. In London, for example, 20% of all open space is occupied by private yards.

Choose your wildlife plant

■ **Crab apples** (*Malus* spp) are ideal for small yards, especially "John Downie" (25 x 25 ft/8 x 8 m) or the weeping M x *scheideckeri* "Red Jade" (12 x 12 ft/4 x 4 m). Insects will gorge on the blossoms and birds love to devour the red or orange fruits.

■ **Hawthorns** (*Crataegus monogyna*) (25 x 25 ft/8 x 8 m) are magnets for caterpillars, which in turn provide food for countless birds. Hawthorns are tough, thorny trees with beautiful white blossoms and bright red berries.

■ **American Mountain Ash** (*Sorbus americana*) (8 x 8 m/25 x 25 ft) also support lots of wildlife. With smooth, orange bark, small, white flowers, and bright red berries in winter.

■ If you don't have space for a tree, but can plant a climber, think about planting an ivy along a fence or wall. **Ivies** (*Hedera* spp) make wonderful curtains of greenery, can be grown on north-facing surfaces, and are top-notch wildlife plants: they are associated with some 230 species of animal, from insects to nesting birds. Ivies are especially valuable as a late source of nectar for butterflies, and the winter berries attract birds. Ivies can be allowed to bush out for an informal look, or clipped to suit a more formally designed plot. If clipping ivy, make sure you wait until after the nesting season, as a secretive wren may have nested there.

■ **Scarlet Firethorns** (*Pyracantha coccinea*) also make excellent evergreen coverings for walls or fences, and their bounty of scarlet or orange berries will feed birds through the cold winter months.

PLANT VEGETABLES IN A "SQUARE FOOT" GARDEN

Even on a patio or balcony, you can grow your own mini vegetable garden with a selection of delicious vegetables—from lettuces to spring onions, radishes to dwarf beans. A "square foot" garden in a sunny patch is easier to manage than a series of pots, makes maximum use of space, and saves on seeds and time spent thinning or weeding—in fact, it's ideal for a novice gardener or for children.

A square foot garden is actually a raised bed. It can be built on top of an area of existing soil, in which case it can be filled with the soil and enriched with garden compost and well-rotted manure. But it can also sit on top of a hard surface, such as pavement, which is the method described here. If you can't fit in a large square (4 ft by 4 ft/1.2 m by 1.2 m) that produces 16 separate "plots," you could make one half this size, which would still give you four squares to grow four different vegetables.

Keep it organic

● Use untreated timber for the box.

● Fill with a mixture of topsoil (from hardware stores or bagged from nurseries), organic compost, and a soil conditioner such as leafmold or garden compost.

● To prevent a build-up of pests and diseases, practice crop rotation: avoid growing vegetables from the same family in the same square for more than one year in three or four.

● Zucchini, sweetcorn, Swiss chard, spinach, and most salads can be grown before or after most other vegetables without problems, and so are very useful in a square foot vegetable garden.

How it works

A square foot garden is contained inside a box or frame made of timber or, if bought ready-made, usually of recycled plastic. A grid dividing the box into 1 ft (30 cm) squares is then laid on top of the soil. This enables you to keep the squares separate so that you can manage the different crops. By keeping the box size 4 ft by 4 ft (1.2 m by 1.2 m), you will be able to reach all the squares without stepping on the soil, which can cause compaction. By using a weed-free nutrient-rich soil mix and planting vegetables closely together, you'll get high yields from your plants and something to pick or snip off right through the season.

■ **Construct a box** using four planks of wood 1¼ in (3 cm) thick and 8–10 in (20–25 cm) high. You need two planks 4 ft (122 cm) long and two planks 3 ft 10 in (116 cm) long. Take one 3 ft 10 in (116 cm) length and onto each end screw one of the 4 ft (122 cm) lengths. Then attach the final 3 ft 10 in (116 cm) length.

■ **Place in a sunny spot**, clear of trees and shade, where it will not puddle after heavy rain.

■ **Fill with soil** (*see* Keep it organic *box*) and make a grid to divide the garden into 1ft (30 cm) squares, either by nailing lengths of cord or string across the area, or with pieces of wood screwed together and laid on top of the soil.

■ **Choose the types of vegetables** you want to eat—you don't have to stick to one square for each type of vegetable: vegetables such as peas, which crop for a longer time if they

Good vegetables to grow

1 Spinach
2 Chard
3 Carrots
4 French beans
5 Lettuce

have more space, would be better grown across two or three squares. Plan to have something to pick right through the summer and into fall. Cut-and-come-again lettuces and herbs will provide you with leaves for many weeks, while herbs such as parsley and oregano can be picked all summer. Avoid slow-growing or deep-rooted crops such as cauliflower or sprouting broccoli. Site taller vegetables, such as beans or peas, at the back where they won't shade out the other squares.

■ **Make a shallow planting hole**, drop in one or two seeds and cover with soil. Water in and leave to germinate. If more than one seedling appears, cut off the weaker one with a pair of scissors so as not to disturb the roots of the remaining plant.

■ **With bushy plants**, like tomatoes, grow one plant per square. With compact plants such as lettuces, or dwarf varieties such as sweetcorn "Honey and Cream," you can fit four per square. With baby vegetables such as the short-rooted carrot "Little Finger," and slim plants such as spring onions or radishes, you can grow up to 16 in one square.

■ **When you have harvested** a fast-maturing crop such as lettuce, you can even plant a second crop of a later vegetable like Swiss chard in the same square.

■ **Refresh the compost**, by digging in well-rotted garden compost or manure, before sowing, the following spring.

COLLECT & USE WATER EFFICIENTLY

In developed countries, we each use three times the amount of water considered sufficient by development agencies for a person's safe and hygienic cooking, washing, and sanitation needs. With climate changes bringing hotter and drier summers, more development on wetland sites, and increased housing needs, water stores—which rely on underground and reservoir water—will soon be severely depleted.

At the moment, the water we use outside only accounts for about six percent of our domestic water use, but the demand for water in our homes is a third higher in summer than in winter—largely because we are watering our plants. In fact, up to 70 percent of the water demand on a summer's evening is due to garden use. And it's expected that the amount we pour onto our gardens will continue to increase. For these reasons, we should try to use less water in the garden, and to water in the most efficient way we can.

One of the best things anyone with outdoor space can do is to store rainwater and use it to water plants and top up water features or bird baths, especially in periods of no rain. Rainwater barrels are widely available in various sizes, shapes, and materials (usually recycled plastic or wood), and many municipalities offer them at discounted prices to encourage gardeners to use them. A barrel can be connected to a down pipe with a simple diverter kit, which also prevents the barrel from overflowing. If you have space, you can even connect a second barrel to the first one, and install others to catch rain from sheds or flat roofs.

How to use a rainwater barrel

■ Stand each barrel on a strong platform—special stands are available—so that you can fit a watering can easily under the tap at the bottom.

■ Put a lid on the barrel to make it childproof, and to keep the water clean and minimize evaporation.

■ Water your plants in the coolest parts of the day and direct the water at the roots.

Water your plants efficiently

■ Add organic matter, such as garden compost or organic soil conditioner, to the soil to improve its structure.

■ Put a layer of mulch, such as bark chips or gravel, around the plants to slow down evaporation from the soil and to suppress weeds.

■ Grow plants that are suited to the conditions in your garden. If it gets very dry and hot in the summer, choose plenty of drought-tolerant plants, which often have silvery leaves and are sometimes downy or waxy. You could also consider creating a rain garden.

■ Use perlite or vermiculite in pots and line them with moss, coir, or perforated plastic.

■ If using containers, choose large ones.

■ For very thirsty plants in containers, push a watering spike into the soil, which releases drops into the soil as and when the plants need moisture.

■ Pour water from a can directly over the root area of each plant in the coolest parts of the day so that most of it does not evaporate.

■ Don't use sprinklers: automatic irrigation systems, such as sub-soil drip pipes that allow water to drip into the soil, make great alternatives to sprinklers, and use far less water. They are especially useful for times when you are out of town.

■ In periods of drought, make use of gray water such as bath, shower, or sink water (which can be distributed to your garden through drip irrigation, or perforated pipe, or collected in containers first). The water should not contain any chemicals. Do not store this water for more than 24 hours and do not use it on plants you intend to eat or come into regular contact with (such as the lawn). You could also make a small depression around each plant to hold moisture after watering or rain falls.

Did you know?

● If you leave a sprinkler on for an hour, it can use the same amount of water that a family of four normally uses in two days.

● Watering during the hottest part of the day can mean that 90% of the water evaporates.

GROW POTS OF TOMATOES

The most delicious summer tomatoes are those that you can pick, sun-ripened, straight from a plant that's growing outdoors—the flavor and aroma are more intense than store-bought ones, or even those raised in greenhouses.

Growing your own tomatoes saves you money—half a dozen plants with good yields should keep a family of four stocked with succulent fruits right through the summer season—and it allows you to grow a range of different and unusual varieties. Choose from cherry-sized salad tomatoes, plums (ideal for sauces), large fleshy varieties such as "Marmande" and even yellow, orange, or striped tomato fruits. Outdoor tomatoes generally have fewer pests and diseases than greenhouse ones and so are easier to manage. In a tiny garden, you can grow them very successfully in pots—the larger the container, the better—or in gro bags or upside-down tomato planters!

Tomatoes grow either as indeterminates—tall, single-stemmed plants also known as cordons, trained to a support and with side shoots and the main growing point removed to speed up ripening—or as determinates, or bush types. Determinates grow from 12–30 in (30 to 75 cm) tall and sprawl out. They don't yield as big a crop as indeterminates, but they are easy to grow and don't need supports or removing flower heads. Dwarf varieties of determinates are often no more than 8 in (20 cm) high, and because they trail they are ideal for window boxes or hanging baskets.

How to grow tomatoes

Tomatoes are tender plants, so they shouldn't be put outdoors while there's a risk of frost. They need a sunny, sheltered spot to ripen, and when grown in containers or gro bags, they need to be regularly watered and fed.

Grow tomatoes from seed

■ Tomato seeds need a minimum temperature of 61°F (16°C) to germinate.

■ Sow them 6–8 weeks before a last frost is due, either in a seed tray or 2–3 seeds to a 3½ in (9 cm) pot or module.

■ Once 2–3 leaves have appeared, transplant the seedlings into individual pots in a light, well-ventilated spot.

■ Harden the seedlings off by leaving them outside for several hours during the day before planting out.

Or buy young tomato plants

■ Buy the plants from a grower or your local nursery.

■ Plant in loam-based compost when the first cluster of flowers (trusses) are visible. Indeterminates need canes or sticks at least 5 ft (1.5 m) tall to support them.

■ As the plants grow, tie the main stems to the supports. Remove any side shoots in mid- to late summer, usually when four trusses have formed, and nip off the main growing point.

Growing tips

● Make sure that your container or pot has sufficient drainage holes.

● Tomatoes in pots and gro bags need regular feeding. Use an organic feed that is rich in potash.

● Water regularly and don't let the plants dry out: add vermiculite or perlite to the compost to help to retain moisture. A container positioned in direct sunlight will require more than two watering cans full of water each day.

● Don't allow the plants to become waterlogged: this can cause the skins of the fruit to split.

● Grow marigolds with the plants to help deter whitefly.

● Pick the fruits as they ripen by snapping them off at the swelling on the stalk, using a thumb and finger. Before the first frosts, take off any unripened tomatoes and store them in a dark, dry place, such as a drawer or in a box in a kitchen cupboard, with an apple or banana. These fruits will give off ethylene, a chemical that accelerates the ripening process.

Choose your tomato plant

Try one, or even two if you have the space, of these varieties, which all grow well in pots or gro bags in a sunny, sheltered site. Other good varieties include Marmande for large fruits and Sungold, which has orange cherry fruits with an excellent flavor.

1 Husky Red Hybrid Dwarf plant, large fruit, extended harvest; determinate.

2 Gold Nugget Yellow fruits; determinate.

3 Gardener's Delight A heavy cropper with deliciously sweet, deep red cherry fruits; indeterminate.

4 Nectar Rose Very tasty salad tomatoes; indeterminate.

5 Tumbler Lots of sweet red fruits; indeterminate.

6 Roma VF Heavy cropping plum; determinate.

7 Tiny Tim Tasty cherry fruits; indeterminate.

8 Big Boy Giant fruits; indeterminate.

9 Pixie Hybrid Small, wonderfully flavored fruits; determinate.

Did you know?

Tomatoes grown in Europe in the 1520s were used as ornamentals since the fruit was thought to be poisonous —the foliage is, in fact, poisonous.

Tomato salad with goat's cheese & basil dressing

(serves four)

If you have a good yield of tomatoes and grow your own salad leaves, try this recipe to bring out the best in your home-grown ingredients.

Ingredients

1½ lb (350 g) vine-ripened tomatoes

4 handfuls mixed salad leaves (rocket, mizuna, frisée, chicory, cress)

1 tablespoon balsamic vinegar

5 fl oz (150 ml) olive oil

A handful of fresh basil

A pinch of salt and black pepper

3 oz (85 g) mild, creamy goat's cheese

Method

■ Cut the tomatoes into chunks and put into a bowl.

■ Place the salad leaves in another bowl.

■ Blend the vinegar, olive oil, basil, and seasoning together to make a thick dressing. Pour half over the tomatoes and carefully mix. Pour the other half over the salad leaves and gently mix.

■ Divide the salad leaves between four plates, top with a serving each of the tomatoes, crumble some of the cheese over each portion, and serve.

GARDEN WITHOUT PESTICIDES

With the possibility that many common garden pesticides have hormone-displacing properties and links to cancer, or can poison pets and wildlife if eaten in large quantities, the safest option is not to use pesticides at all. There are plenty of natural ways to deal with pests, diseases, or unwanted plants or weeds.

To keep pests to a minimum, the first thing you should do is grow your plants well. That means growing them in well-drained, organically fed soil in the right conditions and with the right amount of moisture for each plant. Keeping beds and containers weed-free will give plants the best growing conditions.

Encourage natural predators

There are a whole raft of natural predators at your disposal, from insects, beetles, and birds to frogs, toads, bats, slowworms, and shrews. In order to establish a natural balance in your garden, you will have to tolerate a low level of pests so that the predators have enough to feed on. You also need to think about providing your allies with shelter, other food, and water. Insects generally like to shelter in undisturbed, dark places such as log piles, under stones or a mound of ground-cover plants, or in the hollow stems of plants. They also need a supply of nectar and pollen, which you can provide with a selection of plants. Birds need nesting sites—natural places like thick curtains of ivy or other vines, dense

Tips for natural solutions

● Be prepared to put up with the odd nibbled leaf. An insect such as the leaf cutter bee cuts neat semicircles out of rose leaves for its nest, but it is also a useful pollinator.

● Use your fingers and thumbs to pick off large pests such as caterpillars, lily leaf beetles, or snails (easy to spot at night, with a flashlight) and to knock off aphids from stems and leaves.

● Plant-based insecticides, which break down quickly and don't stay in the environment, are available for organic gardeners, but remember they will kill off other insects, including beneficial ones, as well as the ones you are targeting.

● The best way to avoid diseases is to grow strong, healthy plants in organically managed soil.

● Grow as many different flowering plants with a mixture of flower types as you can and try to make sure there's something in flower right through the season. That way, there'll be nectar and pollen for a wide variety of beneficial insects.

shrubs and trees, or artificial ones—and, depending on the species of bird, food such as seeds, nuts, and berries. Frogs and toads need damp places.

You can also introduce parasitic worms, called nematodes, which occur naturally and target specific pests such as vine weevils, slugs, caterpillars, and leatherjackets. They can be bought in powdered form and usually watered in once the soil reaches a minimum temperature of 41°F (5°C). You may need to apply them twice in a season. Set up barriers to prevent pests reaching seedlings and vulnerable plants (certain plants are beacons for some pests—for example, hostas and dahlias for slugs and snails). Copper tape around pots, or copper mats underneath them, and sharp, dry barriers around plants in the ground can help keep slugs and snails away. Shallow bowls of beer or fruit juice, set just above the surface of the soil so that beetles don't fall in, kill slugs and snails. Collect earwigs, which can polish off young seedlings, in upturned flowerpots filled with straw, and then dispose of them. Organic deer repellents can make your vegetables and fruit unappealing to deer.

Organic allies in the garden

- **Ladybugs** Adults and larvae eat aphids.

- **Hoverflies** Larvae eat aphids.

- **Social wasps** Eat aphids, caterpillars, and flies.

- **Ichneumon wasps** Larvae eat caterpillars, some adults eat aphids.

- **Ground beetles** Eat slugs, snails, and other soil-living creatures.

- **Spiders** Eat aphids and flying creatures.

- **Lacewings** Larvae eat aphids.

- **Tachinid flies** Eat caterpillars and other grubs.

- **Devil's coach-horse beetles** Eat invertebrates.

- **Birds** Species such as grackles, robins, wrens, sparrows, starlings, and blackbirds depend on huge quantities of grubs for their chicks at nesting time. Adult birds such as house sparrows, chickadees, and warblers devour insects, including aphids. Blackbirds, crows, and jays eat slugs and snails.

- **Frogs, toads, and newts** Eat slugs.

GROW SWEET PEAS ON A TEEPEE

One of the most wonderful sights and scents of summer is a vase of freshly picked sweet peas (*Lathyrus odoratus*) in shades of pink, white, yellow, blue, purple, and burgundy. By growing your own, you can pick a bunch every couple of days—and the more you pick, the longer your plants will produce flowers through the summer months.

Sweet peas are climbers, so they need some wires or netting to scramble up a fence or wall, or a tall, free-standing support. In a small outdoor space, you can use a teepee or obelisk in a bed or large pot. The teepee will quickly be covered in the flowers, making a delightful, richly scented feature. Old-fashioned sweet peas have a stronger, spicier fragrance than modern varieties (if you buy modern sweet peas, lavenders, blues, and pale colors are often the most fragrant).

Make a teepee

You can buy ready-made obelisks, but it's much more fun—and cheaper—to make your own using bamboo poles or, for a rustic-style teepee, hazel or willow rods. Annual sweet peas will grow to 6 ft (1.8 m) or more in a season, so the poles need to be 6 ft (1.8–2 m) long. Prepare the soil first (*see left*), then space out six poles to form a circle, pushing them into the ground or the base of a pot and securing them at the top with string or a purpose-made disc, available from nurseries. For extra support, you can weave in some clippings from any flexible-stemmed plants you may have growing, such as clematis, Virginia creeper, or dogwood, or tie in lengths of string.

Sweet peas need

- A sunny, open spot.
- Soil that's had manure or organic compost added to it before planting.
- A good mulch of manure or compost after planting.
- Tying onto the support for the first few weeks of growth.
- Regular watering, especially in dry, sunny weather.
- Picking every couple of days once the flowers appear; once the plants seed they won't produce more flowers.

How to grow sweet peas

You can buy sweet peas as young plants from nurseries and farmers' markets but, if you have time, you can grow your own from seed. Make sure that you choose one of the richly scented varieties—some sweet peas are bred for the shape and size of their flowers—and either sow the seeds under cover in a cold frame or greenhouse in late winter, or outdoors at the foot of the teepee poles in early- and mid-spring.

If growing from seed, there's no need to chip the seed coat (which was the traditional method of preparing them) as long as you soak the potting soil well before burying the seeds in it.

■ Plant just one seed in a 3 in (8 cm) pot, or 6–8 seeds in a 6 in (15 cm) pot or in root trainers. Cover with newspaper until the seedlings appear.

■ When the first four leaves have formed, take off the top two leaves to encourage the plant to bush out. Harden the seedlings off well before planting them out, and be prepared to cover them if there's a cold snap.

■ If you prefer to sow straight into the ground, space out the seeds 8–12 in (20–30 cm) apart.

■ Once the first seedlings appear, or when you have planted out the young plants, tie them onto the support and continue to tie new stems in weekly for the first couple of months. As soon as the first flowers appear, start picking them.

Good varieties of sweet pea

All these old-fashioned varieties will cover a teepee, have masses of small flowers, and are richly scented:

"Black Knight": deep maroon/violet flowers.
"Dorothy Eckford": white flowers.
"Flora Norton": clear blue flowers.
"Henry Eckford": bright orange flowers.
"Lord Nelson": rich, dark blue flowers.
"Matacuna": rich maroon and purple flowers; one of the oldest varieties.
"Mrs. Collier": rich cream-colored flowers.
"Painted Lady": bicolored pink flowers; the oldest variety of sweet pea in existence.

GROW HERBS FOR TEAS & INFUSIONS

Make your own herb teas and infusions from plants growing outside your kitchen window and get the very best flavor, aroma, and healing properties from the freshly picked leaves.

For centuries, herbs have been used to make relaxing or refreshing drinks, and for infusions to help relieve a whole range of ailments from headaches to sore throats and indigestion. You can buy many of these herbs dried, in sachets, from supermarkets and health stores, but the drinks taste much better if you use fresh leaves. Fresh herbs are less concentrated than dried ones, so you'll need to use more (usually twice as much). If you grow them yourself, you'll have plenty of leaves, flowers, and seeds to brew yourself a healthy, non-caffeinated drink—served hot in winter, cool in summer—whenever you feel like it. Many of these herbs have very pretty leaves and flowers, too, so they make excellent plants for window boxes or containers.

Medicinal benefits

Some herbs make pleasant tasting drinks that also have medicinal properties: peppermint, for example, aids digestion. Other herb infusions are mainly taken as natural remedies, such as sage, which has antiseptic properties and can be used as a gargle and mouth rinse. Sage tea can be sweetened with honey and drunk as a remedy for a cold, but can be toxic if over-used.

How to make a herb tea or infusion

Most herb teas have a light, delicate flavor, so two or three teaspoons of fresh leaves are usually enough for a cup of herb tea, although just a single sprig of fresh rosemary in a cup makes a refreshing pick-me-up. Chamomile tea is made from the flowers, which should only be steeped for 3–4 minutes.

● Use freshly picked leaves. Crush the leaves on a piece of kitchen towel to release the oils.

● Put the leaves in a cup or teapot and pour on just-boiled water. Cover tightly and leave to steep for 5–15 minutes, depending on the thickness of the leaves.

Growing tips

- Make sure that the plant pot has at least one drainage hole and a layer of broken clay pieces or gravel at the bottom of the pot.

- Most herbs need a minimum depth of 8 in (20 cm) to grow, but tall plants such as fennel need at least 12 in (30 cm) depth.

- Invasive herbs such as peppermint and lemon balm are best grown alone, as are large plants such as rosemary. Herbs such as sage, thyme, and oregano can be grouped together and grown in one pot.

- Most herbs need well-drained soil, and will collapse if they are waterlogged.

Choose your herbs

Most herbs prefer a sunny position, but many are robust plants and will cope with partial shade, too, so give them a try. Protect the plants from extreme cold and don't let them become waterlogged.

1 Lavender (*Lavandula*)
Pick the flowers just as they open. Use an infusion of flowers for insomnia, loss of appetite, and poor circulation.

2 Fennel (*Foeniculum vulgare*)
Harvest the seeds as they turn brown, and dry them well. Then crush them and add just-boiled water. Use to remedy gas, indigestion, coughs, and bronchitis.

3 Rosemary (*Rosmarinus officinalis*)
Pick leaves all year. Use as a gargle for a sore throat and bad breath. Drink as a tea in small amounts to reduce gas. As an infusion, it conditions hair and makes it shine.

4 Chamomile (*Chamaemelum nobile*)
Pick the flowers just as the petals curl back. Use as a calming drink for indigestion and insomnia. Can be used as a gargle or mouthwash.

5 Hyssop (*Hyssopus officinalis*)
Pick young leaves through the growing season. Use an infusion of leaves for coughs and respiratory congestion. Avoid during pregnancy.

6 Lemon balm (*Melissa officinalis*)
Pick the leaves before the flowers open. Use for headaches and tension, indigestion, and gas.

7 Peppermint (*Mentha spicata*)
Perennial that can be fed with comfrey to give a new crop of tender leaves each year. Use for indigestion, nausea, gas, colds and, served cold, to bring down fevers.

8 Sage (*Salvia officinalis*)
Choose the gray-green non-variegated common sage for the most intense flavor and most potent medicinal properties. Pick leaves throughout the year; they have a milder flavor before flowering. Use as a gargle for sore throats and cold sores. Can also be drunk to soothe indigestion, but should not be taken during pregnancy.

9 Thyme (*Thymus*)
Pick leaves all year round. Use as a gargle for sore throats, sore gums, and cold sores. Also said to be good for hangovers.

MAKE YOUR OWN COMPOST

Even if you only have a small outside space, it's worth thinking about making your own compost. Not only will it take your organic kitchen, household, and yard waste—much of which would otherwise go straight to landfill sites—it also presents you with your own free supply of compost, which you can use to feed and condition the soil and add to potting mixes for plants in containers. If your space is too tiny to fit a composter, check to see if you can send your organic waste to a centralized composting scheme, such as those run by local municipalities or community groups.

The easiest, neatest way to make compost in a small space is in a ready-made compost bin. Most are made from recycled plastic, but if the bin has to be positioned in view, there are also attractive wooden bins available, which can be painted or stained any color you want. Most come without a base so that they can stand on top of the soil—this allows the microorganisms in the soil and larger composting worms and beetles to move up through the material in the bin, composting as they go. If you do not have access to soil, choose a bin with a base and start off with a layer of soil, adding some more if you can as your heap builds up.

There are two ways of making compost: if you have a lot of material to start with, you can go the "hot route:" filling the bin with well-mixed, moistened brown and green matter *(see box, right)* and turning the heap, which will quickly

heat up, several times over a few weeks to speed up the aerobic work of the microbes. You can have dark brown, earthy smelling compost in six to eight weeks. For most people with small yards, and for those with less time on their hands, the "cool route" works best. Place the bin in a warm, sheltered spot.

Cool composting

■ Put a few woody plant stems at the bottom of the bin to help improve air circulation and drainage.

■ Add a good layer of mixed green and brown items *(right)*. Always chop tougher, bigger stems into small pieces. Unless they are already wet, water them with a watering can.

■ Continue filling the bin. Don't put in too much sloppy green waste at once—mix it up with bulkier items.

■ Water the heap if it looks dry.

■ If the heap looks soggy, turn it with a fork and add some more bulky material.

■ The material will eventually rot down. After a few months, check the bottom part. If it looks dark brown and well rotted, dig it out and use in the garden. Mix up the rest, water it if it seems dry, and leave in the bin to continue composting.

The right bin

■ Holds at least 53 gallons (200 liters); the more well-mixed material it contains, the greater the biological activity.

■ Has a lid, to keep rain out and heat in.

■ Has a good-sized opening at the top to fork in yard waste, and is either easy to lift off to get at the compost when it's ready, or has an access door or panel at the bottom.

What to put in

All compost heaps need a mix of "greens"—soft green matter high in nitrogen—and "browns"—tougher plants that take longer to rot and are high in carbon. If you put in a lot of kitchen waste, add bulkier items such as cardboard and egg cartons.

Must-have

Greens and browns
Annual non-flowering weeds
Grass cuttings
Fruit and vegetable scraps
Woody clippings and prunings
Leaves of non-coniferous trees and shrubs such as sycamore, ash, poplar, willow, elm, lime and elder
Sawdust and wood shavings

Also good

Tea bags, coffee grounds, egg shells, and wood ash
Egg cartons, cereal boxes, and other bits of cardboard
Crumpled up paper towels and newspaper
Wool
Old straw and hay, gerbil, hamster, and rabbit bedding

Leave out

Meat, fish, and cooked food
Weed seeds
Diseased plant material
Disposable diapers, dog or cat feces
Glossy newsprint
Coal ash

GROW CHILI PEPPERS IN A POT

Even if you only grow them for the look of their bright, shiny fruits, chili plants can add an exotic element to your patio or balcony in summer. Chilies grow as perennials in their native South America, but they can also be raised as annuals indoors when grown from seed. This means that you can experiment with different varieties—and different degrees of fieriness—to flavor sauces, marinades, and spicy dishes, just for the price of a packet of seeds and some potting soil.

Specialist growers raise chilies in greenhouses or row covers, which provide the plants with the warmth they need for germination and the light for the seedling stage. But you can also start them off on a bright windowsill, as long as the temperature is 70°F (21°C). The easiest way to ensure this is by using a heated mat or propagator. Use a free-draining potting soil, and water well before sowing in small pots. Space a few seeds evenly on the surface of each pot and cover with vermiculite. As soon as the seedlings emerge and are showing two leaves, transfer to small pots (3 in/7.5 cm in diameter) and move them to a spot where they will get plenty of daylight. Keep them warm, moist, and well ventilated. When the plants have five pairs of leaves, transfer into bigger pots. Once there is no danger of frost, harden off the plants by leaving the pots outdoors in a sheltered spot for up to ten days, bringing them in at night. Then leave them outdoors once the nighttime temperature has reached 59°F (15°C).

Chilies in pots need
- Well-drained soil.
- Minimum nighttime temperature of 59°F (15°C).
- Liquid fertilizer every 1–2 weeks once flowers appear.
- Regular picking to encourage more fruit to form.

Hot tips

- The more mature the chili, the hotter it is.

- The white pith, with the seeds attached, is the hottest part.

- The heat is caused by the alkaloid (chemical compound) capsaicin, and the amount each pepper contains varies depending on the variety, soil, climate, and even its position on the plant.

- A chili's heat is measured in Scoville Units. Mild chilies contain about 600 units, while the habaneros types range from 200,000–350,000 units.

- Always avoid touching your eyes or other tender areas after handling chilies. If you have sensitive skin, wear gloves when preparing any chilies.

- If you've eaten too hot a chili, have milk or yogurt.

Good varieties to grow

Filius blue Fruits mature from green to purple to red; medium to hot.

Aurora Fruits mature from green to purple to orange red; very hot.

Cherry bomb Cherry-shaped red fruits; medium hot.

Twilight Green, red, and purple fruits; very hot.

USE RECLAIMED WOOD & FURNITURE

Nowadays, our wood and furniture can be sourced from all over the world. Softwoods such as pine may come from the forests of northern Europe or Russia; tropical hardwoods like teak and mahogany from Africa, Brazil, or Asia. Unfortunately, much of the global timber industry is currently unsustainable. Virgin forests are being clearcut, and plantations are much less valuable for wildlife than the forests they are replacing. Using wood carefully, without waste, is a way of treating this natural product with the respect it deserves.

A new lease of life

The best environmental choice is to repair, restore, or adapt furniture rather than replace it. You may need professional help, but it could still be cheaper than buying new and is far better for the world's forests.

■ Be creative with your existing furniture. An old sofa can be re-covered or livened up with a bright throw. Battered wooden furniture can be stripped and repainted, waxed, stained, or stenciled.

■ Redoing your floor? Check if your existing wooden floorboards can be sanded and used again.

■ If you are discarding furniture, consider selling it or donating to a furniture exchange charity.

■ Buy in antique and secondhand shops.

■ Consider commissioning furniture from professional designers. They can source reclaimed wood and you will get a unique piece of artwork.

Secondhand and reclaimed timber

■ Old wood has a unique beauty. Nowadays, timber trees rarely grow for more than 30 or 40 years.

■ Old timber is more likely to be from a tree that lived for over a century, developing a beautiful dense grain and color.

■ Reclaimed wood is often much cheaper than virgin wood.

Where to find reclaimed wood and reusable furniture

Salvage companies and reclaimed timber merchants. Reclaimed wood can be sourced from remodeled or demolished buildings, disused railroad ties, or even the legs from an old table.

Ads in local papers.

Dumpsters (get permission first).

Your chamber of commerce may have information on timber recycling and furniture exchange schemes.

The facts on wood

● Natural forests are being destroyed to make way for faster-growing "factory forests" for timber and paper production, threatening the survival of many species of trees, plants, and animals. Each year, about 32 million acres of the world's forests are lost to deforestation.

● Deforestation accounts for up to 20% of global CO_2 emissions: vast amounts of carbon are released into the atmosphere when natural forests are destroyed.

● The UN predicts a 58% increase in wood consumption over the next 20 years.

3 YARD, COMMUNITY GARDEN, OR FIELD

KEEP SOME CHICKENS

If you're thinking of keeping livestock for the first time, chickens are a good place to start. They will provide you with a continuing supply of tasty and nutritious eggs, and can be pleasant company.

Chickens are entertaining characters to have around your yard, and are an ideal, low-maintenance introduction to keeping your own birds and animals. Depending on the breed, you can expect to have around 200 eggs or more per year, or tasty, organically reared meat when you want it. Chickens are also the perfect partners in an organic lifestyle. If you grow your own food, you can use a movable chicken run or "ark" to help prepare the ground for sowing. The hens will scratch at the surface of the soil, breaking it up, eat pests and weeds, and apply their own organic fertilizer, which is rich in nitrogen. In return, they are comparatively easy to care for, needing minimal care, grain to eat, somewhere to roam, and housing where they can lay their eggs and roost at night.

Buying your birds

Chickens are available either as hybrids, which have generally been bred to lay larger numbers of eggs, or as pure breeds—the traditional breeds—which are hardier and more disease-resistant, tend to lay eggs from March to September, and can be used for meat. If you buy chicks, you won't be able to tell their sex, which means that you may end up with more than one male bird—you only need a rooster if you want to breed chickens, which is worthwhile if you keep pure breeds. Young hens ready to produce eggs are called pullets, and are usually "at point of lay" at 18–20 weeks old. Look through poultry magazines or contact private breeders for young hens for sale. Ask to see the parent stock before you buy.

It's best to buy just two or three young egg-laying hens to start with. Hens are most productive when they are young, providing a supply of eggs for between two to five years. They lay fewer eggs as they age, so it's worth thinking about slowly introducing a few more hens over time to build a flock that can provide you with a constant supply of eggs.

When new birds arrive, shut them in their own house overnight with some food and water. Gently open the low exit hatch the next morning and, if they find their way out without pressure, they will return to their house again in the evening.

The best way to handle poultry

Handle your hens regularly to check that they are well and haven't lost weight. You can, with practice, use a fishing net to catch a hen, then place both hands around her wings and body and lift her, without squeezing, to face you, talking and moving slowly all the time. Slide one hand under her, rest her weight on your forearm, hold her close to your body and inspect her. Pick up all poultry this way (never hold them upside-down by one leg).

Signs of good health in a chicken

- Dry nostrils.
- Bright eyes.
- A red comb (some breeds have naturally dark combs).
- Shiny feathers (all present).
- Good weight and musculature for age.
- Clean vent (rear-end) feathers with no smell.
- Smooth shanks.
- Straight toes.
- Alert and active.

Top three popular pure breeds

Rhode Island Red

New Hampshire Red

Single-comb White Leghorn

Choose your chickens

Chickens can be bought in two sizes: as small birds, or bantams, and as full-size birds. The lightweight bantams are ideal for a small yard, but the larger birds are usually more docile and sociable. The chickens shown here are all pure breeds, well-suited to free-range life.

Ameraucana
Lays blue eggs. Called "Lavender Araucana" in the UK.

Barred Plymouth Rock
Very good layer of light brown eggs. Easy to keep.

Blue Laced Wyandotte
Large and bantam breeds. Fair layers. Eggs often small.

Appenzeller Spitzhauben
Very active: requires large runs and high fences.

Buff Sussex
Large and bantam breeds. Easy for beginners to keep.

Welsummer
Lays dark brown eggs. Great choice for yards.

Partridge Rumpless Araucana
Lays blue or olive-green eggs. From South America.

Silver Laced Wyamdotte
Lays tinted eggs. Fair layers, but eggs often small.

Rhode Island Red
Lays brown eggs. Good choice for small flocks.

Cuckoo Marans
Lays dark brown eggs. A good table bird.

Gold Penciled Hamburg
Lays white eggs. Requires large runs and high fences.

Light Sussex
Large and bantam breeds. A good table bird.

Hybrid varieties

These hardy breeds are docile, reliable egg layers.

Mrs. Pepperpot
Superb layer of large to extra-large brown eggs. Easy to handle.

Black Rock
Steady layer and disease-resistant. Docile, but full of character.

Speckledy Hen
Easy to handle. Prolific egg layer of dark, chestnut-brown eggs.

Caring for your chickens

Watch your birds every day for signs of ill-health, for example, hens that keep their heads down, eyes closed or refuse to eat, drink, or lay. Check their feed and contact a vet if signs persist. Only treat birds for parasites, such as worms or lice, as they occur. If you are keeping chickens for their eggs, watch out for broody behavior—birds that are reluctant to leave their nest box or become angry when they are disturbed. Remove any eggs and shut them out of their nest box for a few days.

Your hens will molt every fall, becoming quite scraggy—even virtually featherless—from November until February. This is quite normal, and they won't lay during this period.

What you'll need

Hen house A ventilated hen house or coop provides nesting boxes for laying and a place to roost at night, safe from predators. Line the nest boxes with clean straw, and ensure they are in a dark area—hens like dark, secret places to lay their eggs. Clean out the house once a week. Use gloves and a scraper to clean off the droppings and disinfect the floor. Dust for lice every three weeks. If you have broody or new hens, it's a good idea to have another hen house, or section off one area, to separate them for a while.

Free roaming or a run You can allow your hens to wander freely around your yard every day, as they will find their way back to their roost at night. Keep their food and water in their house to deter wild birds. If the chickens are under threat from predators during the day, use a run to protect them, and move it to a new site every so often.

Feed & water Hens need a diet of fresh grain in addition to the insects and seeds they find in the garden. Grit is also essential and should always be available, as it helps them to break down and digest their food. They will also happily feed on green leftovers and cooked rice and pasta (but not meat or fish), from your kitchen. Clear any excess feed away every day to reduce the chances of attracting vermin. Always provide constant supplies of fresh water.

A chicken keeper's kit

1 **Automatic feeders**
will keep food dry.

2 **Fresh water**
Some water containers automatically fill up as the chickens drink from them.

3 **Feed**
Use an organic corn mix and protein pellets from reputable suppliers. Keep food fresh and sealed.

4 **Straw**
Use clean straw, newspaper, or shredded cardboard to line the house.

5 **Hen house**
The house must be vermin-proof and provide 16 sq in (40 sq cm) of space for each hen. Don't use creosote to paint any bird or animal houses, as it is toxic. If you don't want to let your birds run free-range, their run should be as large as possible (ideally 24 sq ft/8 sq m for a few birds) and covered with strong chicken wire. Always keep the hen house clean.

MAKE SIMPLE PRESERVES

Fall provides us with an abundant choice of foods to eat. Preserving some of the harvest means that nothing goes to waste, and extends the season into the winter months when there is less choice. The preserving process transforms flavors and textures, creating complex preserves that will keep for weeks, months, and sometimes even years. Salt, sugar, vinegar, and alcohol can all be used to preserve the foods, which should be sealed in airtight, sterilized mason jars. For safety, do not re-use the lids.

Pickled turnips

Ingredients

3 lb (1.4 kg) turnips, peeled
3 cups (700 ml) white wine vinegar
½ cup (110 g) unrefined sugar
1 tablespoon salt
1 cup (300 ml) olive oil

Method

■ Baby turnips can just be peeled. Large turnips need cutting into neat shapes.

■ Put the vinegar, sugar, and salt into a large stainless steel saucepan and slowly bring to the boil. Add the turnips and simmer for ten minutes.

■ Remove the pan from the heat and allow to cool.

■ Sterilize glass jars and fill with the vegetable

and vinegar mixture. When the jars are almost full, pour a thick layer of olive oil over the top.

■ Seal the jars and store.

Variations

Pickled celery root
Scrub and peel 3 lb (1.4 kg) celery root and cut into wedges. Proceed as above, adding a few celery seeds and a good grinding of black pepper to the jars before covering with olive oil and sealing.

Pickled red bell peppers
Cut 3 lb (1.4 kg) red bell peppers in half, remove the seeds, and cut each half into three. Proceed as above, adding sprigs of rosemary and a bay leaf to each jar before covering with olive oil.

Sauerkraut

Sauerkraut enhances intestinal health, promotes the growth of beneficial intestinal organisms, and improves nutrient absorption. It's also high in antioxidants—especially vitamin C.

Ingredients
2 large white cabbage heads
2 tablespoons salt

Method
■ Finely shred the cabbage with a sharp knife or in a food processor.

■ Put the cabbage in a stainless steel bowl with 1 tablespoon of salt and pound well until some of the juices start to flow. The flat end of a wooden rolling pin is excellent for this job. Loosely cover with a cloth and leave for 24 hours.

■ Rinse out a 3½ pint (2 liter) glass jar. Put about 2 in (5 cm) of cabbage in the bottom of the jar, sprinkle with a little of the remaining salt, and press down firmly. Continue until the cabbage is used up, leaving some space at the top of the jar (the cabbage will expand during fermentation).

■ Cover the mouth of the jar with greaseproof paper and place a weight on top. This weight forces water out of the cabbage, and then keeps the cabbage submerged under the brine until the sauerkraut is ready to be eaten. Some cabbage may not contain a lot of water. If the brine doesn't rise above the weight level after one day, add a little water to cover the cabbage.

■ Let the jar sit in a well-ventilated space at room temperature. After a week, the cabbage will have fermented sufficiently to be eaten.

■ Cover the top with a plate and store in the fridge, where it will last for at least one month.

Variations
Caraway & coriander sauerkraut
Grind 1 tablespoon of mixed caraway and coriander seeds in a pestle and mortar or other grinder. Mix the seeds with the cabbage before layering in the jar.

Seaweed sauerkraut
Replace the salt with a handful of dried seaweed (approx 1 oz/25 g). Cut into small pieces, soak in warm water to rehydrate for 30 minutes, then drain well. Proceed as above, but fill the jar with alternate layers of cabbage and seaweed.

Pumpkin & apricot chutney

Ingredients

1 cup (250 g) red onions, chopped

A large chunk of fresh root ginger, grated

3 cloves of garlic, finely chopped

1 large chili, finely chopped

2 tablespoons olive oil, plus a little for roasting

A large pinch each of cumin powder, coriander powder, salt, and pepper

1½ cups (300 g) dried apricots, whole

2 cups (500 ml) cider vinegar

1½ cups (300 g) unrefined sugar

½ cup (200 g) sultanas

1 cup (250 ml) water

1 bay leaf

1 lb (500 g) pumpkin, peeled, and cubed

Method

■ In a thick-based pan, cook the onions, ginger, garlic, and chili in the olive oil until tender.

■ Add the rest of the ingredients, except the pumpkin, to the pan and bring to the boil. Simmer for one hour, stirring occasionally.

■ Meanwhile, toss the pumpkin cubes in a little olive oil and roast in a hot oven until they have taken on some color and are soft.

■ Add the pumpkin to the chutney and simmer for a further 10 minutes. Remove from the heat.

■ Sterilize some glass jars and fill with the chutney. Fasten the lids securely and store in a cool, dry place for up to six months.

HEAT WATER NATURALLY

A quarter of the energy used in our homes is required to heat water. During the summer, and for a surprising number of winter months, too, that water could be heated by the sun. Harnessing the sun's power is an easy way to minimize your household carbon emissions while maximizing your use of a free and renewable supply of energy.

The benefits of "solar thermal collectors," as the rooftop panels that heat water using the sun's energy are called, are numerous: they require very little maintenance; they have virtually no running costs; they usually only take a day to install; and, in some cases, you don't require building permits.

How do I find a solar thermal collector?

There are now quite a few solar thermal collector manufacturers, but it's worth shopping around. Most companies will send a licensed installer to your home to give you a quote based on your specific needs. Another option is to install a solar thermal collector yourself. Many energy organizations, and even manufacturers themselves, give short courses on installation and maintenance.

How does it work?

■ The solar thermal collector is installed on your rooftop. South-facing roofs pitched at a 35–40° angle are preferable, but not strictly necessary.

■ Heat from the sun is absorbed and retained by insulated tubes. The tubes are designed to work even with minimal sunlight available.

■ Water, directed from the water main, passes through the tubes and is heated up.

■ The hot water is piped into your water storage tank where it is stored until needed.

■ During the summer months, a collector will supply practically all your hot water.

■ Throughout the rest of the year, the collector works alongside your water heater to heat water, but enables you to rely less on your boiler.

NOURISH THE SOIL

Although some plants, especially annual weeds, can take root and thrive with hardly any nutrients or water in scrapings of dusty soil, most garden plants need good soil to grow strong and well. Making sure the soil has a good structure and a supply of nutrients is the most important thing to do before planting, and it will save you having to feed plants in beds and borders once they're established. Plants grown on a healthy diet of naturally enriched soil are less prone to pests and diseases, too.

It's useful to know the natural acidity of your soil so that you can grow plants best suited to your conditions and, where needed, make alterations to the soil. Acidity and alkalinity is measured on a pH scale from 0 to 14, 0 being the most acid and 7 being neutral. Certain plants—like ericaceous rhododendrons and heathers—thrive on acid soil, but most crops need a neutral to slightly acid soil, with a pH of about 6.5. Adding lime (ideally slow-acting ground limestone) or calcified seaweed in late fall can raise the pH. Digging in organic matter, especially composted pine needles, can help to neutralize an over-alkaline soil. You can easily check your soil's pH using a soil-testing kit.

Here's a checklist of things you can do to give your plants the best possible growing conditions.

■ **Add bulky organic materials to the soil** These improve the soil's structure, increasing drainage on heavy soils and water retention on light soils, and also feed microscopic creatures,

Digging tips

● Only dig the soil if you need to improve its structure.

● Try not to mix topsoil and subsoil—subsoil is a different color from topsoil.

● Don't dig when the ground is frosted or very wet.

● Try not to walk on the soil, especially when it's wet, as this can compact it and damage the structure. Work from a plank of wood, which spreads your weight, if necessary.

What goes in a composter?

Yes

● Green matter such as fruit and vegetable scraps, weeds, and grass cuttings.

● Brown matter such as leaves of non-coniferous trees and shrubs such as sycamore, ash, poplar, willow, elm, lime, and elder, cardboard including cereal boxes and egg cartons and brush, etc.

● Organic material such as tea bags, coffee grains, egg shells, wood ash, wool, straw, pets' bedding, kitchen towels, and newspaper.

No

Meat, fish, and cooked food
Weed seeds
Diseased plant material
Disposable diapers and animal feces
Glossy newsprint
Charcoal ash

which then make nutrients available to the plants. To improve poor soil, fork plenty of compost or other organic materials into the top 6–8 in (15–20 cm) of soil. Choose from garden compost, green waste composts, mushroom compost, leafmold, well-rotted manures, straw, and hay. Fresh horse or cow manure should be mixed with bedding material such as straw or hay and left to mature for at least a month. This converts the nitrogen and potassium in the manure into forms that the plants can use, and allows any chemical residues to be broken down. Manures and other composts can be bought at nurseries, municipal sites, or specialist suppliers, but leafmold and garden compost are easy to make, save waste being sent to landfills, and cost nothing aside from the materials for the composters.

■ **Mulch** Mulching involves putting a generous layer of organic material on the surface of the soil, leaving space around the stems of the plants. This should be done when the soil is warm and wet. Mulch helps to keep the soil moist and to protect the structure of the soil at the surface. It is eventually incorporated into the topsoil, where it is decomposed by the action of worms and other soil creatures.

■ **Grow green manures** These are fast-growing plants, such as clover (*Trifolium* spp) and Phacelia tanacetifolia, that protect bare soil, especially over winter on a vegetable plot, and can be dug in to improve its structure and fertility before planting.

■ **Add organic fertilizers** Organic fertilizers such as bonemeal or rock phosphate are useful when planting new shrubs and trees, or where the soil is poor. Poultry litter, or manure, provides nitrogen, phosphates, potash, and calcium. Comfrey and chopped kudzu vines will release trace elements and minerals over several months and can be added to the soil or to potting soil. Once your soil has been improved, many plants, especially trees and shrubs, will not need regular feeding.

How to make garden compost

Compost is made when organic matter is broken down by bacteria. It needs an insulated composter—you can make your own from pieces of wood, or buy a ready-made one in recycled plastic or wood—with a lid or covering, such as a piece of old carpet, to keep the contents warm and the rain out.

A composter should be placed on soil so that the soil micro-organisms and composting creatures such as worms can get to work. Fill it with a mixture of green matter—soft materials such as grass clippings, fruit and vegetable peelings, and weeds—and tougher brown matter, such as brush and cardboard. Keep the heap moist, but not waterlogged. You can make compost in two ways, but for either, the material should be cut into small pieces.

To get high-speed compost, the compost heap needs to heat up. The best way to achieve this is to fill the composter with well-mixed, well-watered materials all at once, and then leave it for a week or two while it heats up. When it starts to cool, mix it up to introduce more oxygen, then cover it to let it heat up again. You may need to do this several times, but you should be able to use the dark brown, crumbly composted matter in six to eight weeks. This is a great method if you have time to do the turning, and have space for another one or two composters to take your new garden and kitchen waste in the meantime.

Did you know?

When dead plant material is broken down by soil animals and microorganisms, it forms humus, which slowly releases minerals into the soil and makes nutrients available for plants. Humus can remain in the soil for hundreds of years.

In a healthy soil, the organic humus and mineral particles stick together to form tiny crumbs a millimeter or so thick. These crumbs are held together by electrical attraction, and by organic "glues" produced by bacteria. The tiny pores in between this crumb structure form a kind of "sponge" that helps to retain water in the soil.

With the slower, cooler method, start off the composter with a 12 in (30 cm) layer of mixed matter and add to it when you can. Don't put in too much of one thing: kitchen scraps should be mixed with bulkier pieces of cardboard or scrunched-up paper, and grass clippings with coarser bits of plants. If the heap becomes too wet, fork in some bulky woody matter or cardboard. A handful of ground agricultural limestone stops the heap from becoming acidic, which slows down decomposition. Check the bottom section of the heap after several months and any dark, well-rotted matter can be dug out ready for use. Then mix up the remaining material, water if necessary, and return it to the composter.

How to make leafmold

Quantities of leaves are best recycled separately, as they rot down slowly—mainly by the action of fungi. Gather up fall leaves and water them if they are dry. Pack them into recycled or biodegradable plastic garbage bags, tie them, make a few holes in each bag, and store out of the way somewhere. After one to two years, depending on the leaves, the leafmold will be crumbly to the touch and rotted enough to be used as a mulch or soil improver. If left longer, it will decompose further and be fine enough to use in seed-sowing or potting soil.

MAKE FRESH JUICES

If you have a glut of fruit and vegetables, turn them into healthy, refreshing juices. Apples, carrots, and pears are all high in antioxidants and are good sources of vitamin A (carrots) and vitamin C (apples). Apple juice is also known to be cleansing and beneficial to the liver and gall bladder.

Apple, pear & ginger juice
(serves 1)

Apples and pears blend well together, while ginger adds a warming, pungent flavor. This is good to drink if you have indigestion or nausea.

Ingredients
1 apple
1 pear
1 small cube of fresh root ginger

Method
■ Wash the fruit (don't peel or core it) and cut it into small enough chunks to fit in the juicer.
■ Juice the fruit pieces, along with the ginger.
■ Pour into a glass and drink immediately.

Apple, carrot & beetroot juice

(serves 1)

This fresh juice is a blood-building, nutrient-rich, energy provider.

Ingredients

1 apple

1 carrot, medium

1 beetroot, medium

Method

■ Wash the apple and scrub the carrot and beetroot well. Cut up into small enough chunks to fit into the juicer's feeder.

■ Juice the ingredients and drink immediately.

GROW YOUR OWN VEGETABLES

Depending on how much space you have to spare and how much time you can give to tending them, growing your own vegetables can keep you supplied with ready-to-pick crops all year round. Alternatively, it can offer you the chance to grow some unusual varieties that might be expensive to buy. Either way, the flavor and freshness of what you grow can provide you with the ingredients for a succession of gourmet meals.

If you've never grown vegetables before, it's a good idea to start off with just a few varieties—string beans, potatoes, spinach, chard, zucchini, pumpkins, and onions are all pretty straightforward to grow, especially if you buy them as young plants. However, if you want to dedicate several beds or plots to raising vegetables, then it's worth doing some planning first.

Where to grow

Vegetables grow best in a light, open spot in well-drained soil enriched with plenty of organic matter, and with a pH (this measures the acidity of a soil) of around 6.5. A few vegetables, such as beet, kale, spinach, and radish can cope with light shade, but most crops need at least six hours of full light a day.

The plants also need moisture to enable their rapid growth, so they won't thrive next to a big hedge or tree. If you plan to grow "thirsty" vegetables, such as leafy (spinach, salads, summer cabbage) or fruiting kinds (tomatoes, zucchini, peas, beans), then make sure that there is good access to a water supply. All vegetables also need good air circulation, but in windy sites, they may require some protection.

What to grow

It's worth doing some research into the vegetables that you would like to grow and eat. Half-hardy tomatoes, cucumbers, sweetcorn, eggplant, and sweet peppers need warm summer temperatures to crop, while cauliflower is not a good choice for sandy soils. Maincrop vegetables need several months of growing before they are ready to pick, while quick-growing kinds, such as radish, spinach, rocket, spring onions, chard, and cut-and-come-again salads, can be harvested in a few weeks and provide pickings before and after maincrops. Long-term vegetables, such as asparagus and rhubarb, are better planted in a plot of their own where they can grow undisturbed.

How to grow

Traditionally, vegetables are grown in long rows with narrow paths for access, but this method tends to be time consuming, and the soil in between the rows can become compacted. Growing vegetables in equal-sized beds, with a generous path around each one, enables you to do all the digging and weeding from the path, and the vegetables to be planted close together. This method gives high returns and is easier to manage. The beds can be made flat on the soil, or raised and contained within a neat edging made of timber planks.

Planning tips

● If you only have a small space for vegetables, or find it difficult to work out a rotation plan with the vegetables you want to grow, stick to just one rule: don't follow crops from a particular family group with ones from the same group, especially if the crop you've just grown has done badly.

● Try to include some vegetables that will provide you with pickings over many weeks. Good crops to choose include leeks, purple-sprouting broccoli, and parsnips. Quick-growing crops, such as loose-leaf lettuce, spinach, and radish, sown at intervals of a few weeks, give the same effect.

● Make good use of space by following early crops such as potatoes with half-hardy ones such as quick-growing salads, or zucchini and sweetcorn.

Crop rotation

Traditionally, the key to successful vegetable growing, especially the organic way, is crop rotation. This involves planting vegetables in family groups, and ensuring that each group is not grown in the same bed or part of the plot for at least three years.

The main reason for this rotation method is to avoid the build-up of pests and diseases, which attack plants that are botanically related. Crop rotation also helps to keep a balance of nutrients in the soil—legumes, for example, release nitrogen into the soil and so are good crops to grow before brassicas, which need high levels of nitrogen. The rotation system also helps to control weeds: some crops, such as pumpkins and potatoes, have lots of leafy cover that suppresses weeds; others, such as carrots, allow weeds to germinate easily.

Make a plan for a three- or four-year rotation of your beds or plot. Number the beds and allocate a family group to each one. Then decide which vegetables within each group you would like to grow. The carrot and potato families are often grouped together. Work out how many weeks or months each vegetable will be in the ground and choose others to grow before or after, where possible.

Main vegetable families for crop rotation

■ **Brassicas** (*Brassicaceae/Cruciferae*) Some in this group are quick-growing vegetables, such as radish, salad rocket, and salad mustard. Most, such as broccoli, brussel sprouts, cabbage, calabrese, cauliflower, kale, and turnip, are in the ground for several months, and it is these crops that need to be rotated.

■ **Legume** (*Leguminosae*) beans, peas, green manures such as clover.

■ **Potato** (*Solanaceae*) potatoes, eggplants, peppers, tomatoes.

■ **Onion** (*Alliaceae*) onions, leeks, garlic, shallots.

■ **Carrot** (*Umbelliferae*) carrots, celery, parsnips.

Other vegetables, such as members of the beet family *(Chenopodiaceae)* like Swiss chard and spinach beet, members of the daisy family *(Compositae)* such as lettuce, and vegetables such as sweetcorn can be grown in any bed or part of the plot, often before or after the main crop.

Planning a three-year crop rotation scheme

With a rotation scheme, the crops return to their original beds after a break of three to four years.

List all the vegetables you want to grow over a season, and the approximate numbers of plants required for each crop.

Divide the vegetables into groups *(see suggestions, below left)*.

Perennials

If you intend to grow perennial crops, such as asparagus, rhubarb, and artichokes, you should grow them in the same plot for several years, as they take time to establish. Perennial herbs like rosemary can also be grown in this bed.

Rotation group A This group could contain green, leafy brassicas *(see left)*. These plants do best in a slightly alkaline soil (pH 6.5–7), so you may need to apply some lime well before planting.

Rotation group B Legumes, which help to fix nitrogen in the soil, could make up this group *(see left)*. This plot may need general fertilizing early in the growing season.

Rotation group C This group could comprise the potato, onion, and carrot families *(see left)*. Of all the groups, this has the highest feeding requirements. Nourish the soil with organic fertilizers, compost, or well-rotted manure.

Move the groups from bed to bed each year *(see diagram, right)*. It's a good idea to let the brassica group (A) move into the plot that's just had legumes (B) growing in it, so that there will be plenty of available nitrogen in the soil for these leafy crops.

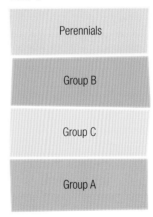

Year 1

Perennials

Group A

Group B

Group C

Year 2

Perennials

Group C

Group A

Group B

Year 3

Perennials

Group B

Group C

Group A

USE RENEWABLE ENERGY

The simplest way to use renewable energy at home is to switch to a green electricity provider, but if you want to take your green commitment further and the idea of being energy independent appeals, become your own electricity supplier. Microgeneration schemes exist to harness the endless, natural supplies of power from the wind, sun, water, and earth.

Those who choose to be energy pioneers are usually looking for more than a quick payback on their energy bills, and it must be said that while off-grid technologies are developing quickly, there still isn't an economic argument for generating your own electricity. By opting for small-scale, decentralized electricity generation, however, you'll become part of the building block of a future power grid.

Microgeneration schemes

Before focusing on your supply, minimize your energy demands (check the energy efficiency of your heating, lighting, insulation, and electrical appliances).

While some microgeneration schemes come close to fulfilling a household's energy needs, it is prudent to have a fall-back option. Most schemes work in tandem with an existing grid connection, which switches on in times of intermittent supply (as in wind and sun) or at peak usage times. This can also work in your favor—if your demand is low and you produce more electricity than you need, you could sell it back to a main grid.

How to get "unplugged"

Micro wind turbines

Turbines use the wind's forces to turn blades that power a rotor to create electricity. They can be small enough to fit onto a roof and big enough to stand alone on top of a hill or in a field. Wind speed increases with height, so it's worth checking out the wind speeds of your site before going any further. In urban areas in particular, turbines might not pick up enough wind to be viable.

Solar panels

Photovoltaic solar panels cells convert the sun's radiation into electricity and, like solar thermal collectors (which heat water), are a free source of energy sitting on your roof. A solar panel could provide up to half your electricity needs through the year.

Ground source heat pumps

Heat from deep underground is extracted through pipes connected to a heat pump, which converts it into high-grade heat for radiators and hot water. You will need to power the heat pump, but you can expect a 4:1 return on the amount of electricity generated.

Hydro power

If you live near a natural water source such as a stream or river, you could use the power from running water to drive a turbine or a water wheel to produce electricity. Depending on the flow rate of the water, microhydro sites can generate enough power for all the electrical appliances in a household.

Green energy suppliers

Electricity production is the single biggest contributor to the emissions that cause climate change.

Across the United States, electricity companies are offering alternative energy options to their customers. For example, many customers can now choose to buy wind power to provide for part, or all, of their domestic electricity needs. Although wind power is slightly more expensive than traditional electricity, customer demand will surely bring prices down in the future—as well as increasing the number of environmentally-sustainable energy options available.

PLANT A FRUIT ORCHARD

What could be more enjoyable than an orchard that you've planted yourself? Walking in the dappled shade of blossom-laden fruit trees in spring to the sound of pollinating bees, watching fruits swell on the trees in summer, and picking your own sun-ripened harvest are all experiences not to be missed.

Orchards are special places, and were highly valued in medieval times as gardens in their own right—offering shade, enclosure, tranquillity, and, of course, nutritious fruits. With so much of the fruit that we eat nowadays coming from miles (even air miles) away and picked before it is beginning to ripen, you may wonder why we have allowed so many orchards to die out or be felled for intensive agriculture or land development. An orchard offers you the chance to eat your own ripe fruit and choose from an array of wonderful varieties that aren't available in stores. All have their own distinctive flavors and crop successively through the summer and fall. An orchard is also a magnet for wildlife, especially pollinating insects such as bees and hoverflies, birds such as redwing blackbirds, butterflies, and small mammals, which all feed on fallen fruit. Once the trees mature, countless invertebrates and insects will feed on and live in any dead wood, and birds such nuthatches, woodpeckers, and tree creepers will nest in hollow trunks.

What you need

Space For a modest-sized orchard, allow enough room to grow at least six standard trees (with trunks at least 6 ft/1.8 m high) or half-standard trees (with trunks 4½ ft/1.4 m high). The branches of one tree should not touch any neighboring branches when fully grown. This means that a vigorous standard apple should be planted at least 28–30 ft (9–10 m) from its neighbors. You can also grow dwarf trees, often seen planted in crowded rows in commercial orchards, but these do not produce the special sense of place that a traditional orchard filled with tall, airy trees creates. How close you space them depends on the eventual size of the tree, the kind of fruit tree you plant, and the planting patterns in your region.

Well-drained soil Don't plant in soil that is prone to waterlogging.

Shelter Trees need protection from prevailing winds—plant windbreaks if the site is exposed. Don't plant in a frost pocket. In areas that are prone to frost, plant late-flowering varieties.

What to grow

Apples and pears are popular choices, but cherries, plums, and damsons can all make up your orchard. What you grow depends on what fruits you want to pick for your household, and which varieties are particularly suited to your conditions and the area that you live in. Cherries, for example, do best in sheltered areas where the rainfall is light. They can make majestic trees—up to 40 ft (12 m) tall—and require plenty of space. All varieties of plum tree flower in spring, so they should be grown in a frost-free site, if possible.

Apple trees can be grown in most places, but before you buy your trees, do get advice from your local supplier on three things: the rootstock, the most appropriate variety, and pollination needs. Apples and pears are grafted onto rootstocks that determine the eventual size of the tree, the age when it starts to fruit, and the amount of fruit it can produce. Rootstock M111 will produce a vigorous, wide-spreading standard tree that will start to produce fruit after six

years or so. MM106 is used for half-standard trees that bear fruit after four years or so.

A few fruit trees are self-pollinating—they can set fruit with their own pollen—but most need one or more other varieties of the same fruit tree, growing no further than 60 ft (18 m) distance away, to pollinate them. Wind and insects such as bees transfer the pollen from the flowers of one tree to another. Apple trees, for example, are listed in four different pollination groups (A–D) based on their flowering season. Varieties can be pollinated by others in the same pollination group, or in the group just before or after.

Use growers' catalogs to help you make your choice. There are hundreds of varieties to choose from, with different flowering and harvesting times and distinctive flavors and textures, and some are particularly disease-resistant.

Planting & caring for your trees

Orchards certainly don't need to be manicured, but they do need to be cared for, especially in the first few years, in order to produce healthy trees that provide plenty of juicy, vitamin-packed fruits.

Bare-root trees, which are cheaper and easier to plant, should be planted in winter or early spring when the tree is dormant, in frost-free soil. Container-grown trees can be planted any time, but they will establish better if they are planted in the winter. If you know how to prune a fruit tree, buy a one-year-old feathered maiden (a tree that has a central stem with a number of lateral branches off it). If not, buy a two- or three-year-old tree that has been trained by the grower.

■ **Mark out** the planting area with a pole and measure out the required distance from one tree to the next.

■ **Prepare the soil** before planting, adding plenty of organic matter if the soil is sandy or heavy. Mix some bonemeal into the soil in each planting hole. Put in a short stake on the side of the prevailing wind (although this is not necessary if you are planting a maiden tree), and make sure that the place where the rootstock and grafted stem are joined will be positioned well above ground level. Water in the tree and keep well-watered during the first year or two—drought stress is a common cause of death in young trees.

Did you know?

About 2,500 varieties of eating and cooking apples have been cultivated in the United States, with only about 100 of those being grown commercially.

Pears are slower to start fruiting than apples, but can produce fruit for up to 300 years.

Researchers say that eating two apples a day can lower cholesterol levels by 10%.

It takes nearly 40 apples to make one gallon of cider.

Apples float because 25 percent of their volume is air.

■ **Mulch** an area of at least 1 m (3 ft) in diameter around each tree with well-rotted manure, garden compost, straw, or wood chippings, but don't let the mulch touch the trunk. Keep mulching the area, and ensure it is kept weed-free, for the first three to four years (every year if the soil is poor).

■ **Fit a tree guard** if there are likely to be grazing animals in the orchard: attach the tree to the stake with a tie made of strong, flexible material.

■ **Prune each winter** for the first four or five years, cutting back branches to make a framework of strong, well-spaced branches. Once the tree has developed its framework, all it needs is light pruning in order to take out any dead and diseased wood or crossing branches.

■ **Remove all blossoms** in the first spring after planting.

■ **Feed** with an organic fertilizer in early spring.

■ **Encourage natural predators**—chickadees, ladybugs, and lacewings will pick off aphids, while underplanting with chives or garlic will help to deter them. Nectar-rich flowers, such as wildflowers, will attract pollinating insects.

■ **Check the tie** every six months or so, and loosen it if it is too tight. Once the tree roots are well-established—usually after one to two years—remove the tie and take out the stake.

Choose your apple trees

How well a tree crops depends on the location and health of the tree. Some, such as Bramley's Seedling and Holstein, can have a less productive season every second year or so. Good apple varieties to try include:

1 Egremont Russet
A classic russet with rough skin, crisp flesh, and a sweet flavor. Young trees crop heavily, but mature ones can become irregular.

2 Kidd's Orange Red
A sweet dessert apple, similar to Cox's Orange Pippin, that crops heavily and has quite good resistance to disease. Keeps November to January.

3 Lord Lambourne
A compact tree with medium-sized, red-flushed dessert apples that are sweet and juicy. Crops heavily.

4 Discovery
A bright red early dessert apple with crisp flesh. The blossom is tolerant of frost and the medium-sized fruits keep well.

5 Arthur Turner
A traditional British variety. A large cooker with a dry texture that is good for baking. Crops heavily.

6 Ashmead's Kernel
One of the best late dessert apples, with crisp flesh and an excellent flavor. Cropping is light. Keeps December to February or March.

7 Pixie
Bears small dessert apples that are yellowish green flushed with red, and which are crisp and juicy. Crops heavily.

8 Sunset
A smallish, coxlike dessert apple that is easy to grown and crops well. Tolerates a moist climate.

9 Winter Gem
A late dessert variety that bears large red-flushed apples with an excellent flavor. Keeps November to February.

Varieties that crop generously

Alkmene (also called Early Windsor)
Arthur Turner (cooker)
Bramley's Seedling (cooker)
Discovery
Egremont Russet
Elstar
Falstaff
George Cave
Kidd's Orange Red
Kent
Limelight
Lord Derby (cooker)
Lord Lambourne
Red Windsor
Scrumptious
Sunset
Winter Gem

Varieties that store well for several months

Ashmead's Kernel
Bramley's Seedling (cooker)
Claygate Pearmain
Laxton's Superb
Orleans Reinette
Pixie
Tydeman's Late Orange
Winter Gem

GROW YOUR OWN RASPBERRIES

Raspberries are some of the most delicious and nutritious summer fruits—they're rich in vitamin C and good for your immune system. Since raspberries are delicate to handle and will spoil in hot conditions or if wet, the varieties that are sold in supermarkets are bred to be firm and long-lasting, and so are not necessarily the most delicious. If you grow your own, you can pick the berries just before eating them, and by planting a range of succulent summer- and fall-fruiting types you will have a supply of berries from midsummer through to the first frosts. Ask for some spare canes from a gardening friend who has good, disease-free plants and you can save yourself even more money.

Raspberry canes continue cropping for up to ten years. Although they do best in full sun, they can cope with some shade (unlike most other fruits). The small, white flowers attract bees and other pollinating insects and the berries make feasts for birds, so either grow some extra canes to allow for bird raids or protect the plants with fine netting.

For the best crops, grow your raspberries in well-drained, well-fed (not chalky) soil, keep them well-mulched and watered and prune them at the right time of year.

How to grow raspberries

The plants are sold as bundles of rooted canes, or rooted in containers. Plant in late winter in soil fed generously with garden compost or well-rotted manure. Most fall-fruiting varieties have short canes and don't need support, but summer fruiters can reach 10 ft (3 m) high, so use wooden posts (10 ft/3 m high) set into the ground at 10 ft (3 m) intervals.

Varieties to try

All Gold Fall-fruiting yellow berries with sweet flavor.

Autumn Bliss Fall-fruiting large, firm red berries.

Glen Ample Midsummer fruits: large red berries, spine-free stems.

Glen Magna Late summer fruits: large red berries, good disease resistance.

Malling Admiral Late summer fruits: sweet red conical berries, good disease resistance.

Malling Jewel Early summer fruits: firm, dark red berries that ripen slowly. Compact growth.

Tulameen Late summer fruits: large, sweet berries with long picking season.

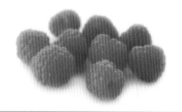

■ Plant the canes in rows, allowing 36 in (90 cm) between each row. Support the canes with horizontal wires fixed to the posts: fix screws to the posts at 30 in (75 cm), 3½ ft (1.1 m) and 5 ft (1.5 m) intervals from the ground, then attach strong galvanized wire so that it's taut. Plant the canes 16 in (40 cm) apart, spreading out the roots and firming the backfilled soil.

■ Prune the canes to 10 in (25 cm) once planted. In the spring, weed well, mulch with garden compost, and add an organic fertilizer.

For summer-fruiting varieties

■ These types produce fruit on canes that appeared the previous year. In midsummer, cut down the original cane (there's usually just one per plant) to ground level. Thin out new shoots to about three to six per plant to prevent overcrowding.

■ In early fall, cut down the canes that have fruited. Tie in young canes that have grown since midsummer to the wires.

■ In winter, add a layer of garden compost to the soil.

For fall-fruiting varieties

■ In the summer, tie in the canes but don't cut down the original cane—it will produce fruit later in the year.

■ In the fall, pick the ripe berries until the first frosts.

■ In the winter, cut all the canes down to ground level and protect with a layer of garden compost.

Tips

● Raspberries like cool, moist summers. In hot, dry climates and conditions, autumn-fruiting types will do better.

● Don't let the roots of bare-rooted plants dry out. Plant them as soon as possible.

● Keep the plants weed-free, but hoe carefully as they have shallow roots.

● Hoeing gently round the canes in winter helps to expose overwintering pests, such as the raspberry beetle, so that birds can get at them.

● Thinning the canes to allow the air to circulate will help to protect against diseases.

● If you have a glut of fruit, freeze the berries.

● Pick the berries on a dry day; any moisture on the fruit will cause it to turn moldy.

USE A WOOD-BURNING STOVE

Burning wood can be a very efficient source of energy in the home, but much depends on how the wood is being burned. Open fireplaces, while very cosy on a winter's night, allow most of the heat to vanish up the chimney. A step up is a wood burning stove. Fueled by either logs, wood shavings, sawdust, or corn or wood pellets, it requires a third of the fuel of an open fireplace and is up to 70 percent more efficient.

In addition to wood burning stoves, a range of wood-fueled boilers are also now available that are as efficient as modern furnaces—converting over 90 percent of the fuel into heat. Compared to a conventional furnace, it does take effort to keep wood burners fed, and log stoves need to be refueled every day, but wood chip or corn or wood pellet stoves can be automated to control temperature settings and only need refilling every few days.

Wood fuel

Buying wood fuel, unless you have your own source, will be an ongoing cost, but bought in bulk it is usually less expensive than fossil fuels. It's important to ensure that the wood fuel has a low moisture content: the more moisture it contains, the more inefficiently it burns, and damp wood can emit high levels of pollutants.

As the technologies for using wood as a fuel have advanced, so has the realization that wood is a suitable alternative to fossil fuels. It is widespread, renewable, and "carbon neutral"—meaning that when it is burned it releases only the amount of carbon dioxide it absorbed while it was growing. Not only that, unlike oil and gas, wood can usually be sourced locally.

GROW FLOWERS FOR CUTTING

In the developed world, especially in North America, Western Europe, and Japan, we love to buy cut flowers for our homes, work places, as gifts, or for special occasions. Over 50 million roses are given worldwide on Valentine's Day alone. Many of these cut flowers are transported long distances by air to reach the flower markets as swiftly as possible, and contribute to the problem of increased carbon dioxide emissions.

Cut flowers are also treated with a number of different pesticides, fungicides, and fumigants to ensure blemish-free blooms. These chemicals create health problems in many of the countries where the flowers are intensively grown, both for the workforces who may not be properly protected as they work, and in the wider environment where the harmful chemicals can contaminate waterways.

Pure blooms

It's possible to avoid contributing to these problems by growing your own flowers for cutting. With a little planning, you can grow a variety of flowering plants that will provide enough beautiful blooms to fill a vase or two every week from spring through to fall. By growing your flowers organically—using plenty of organic matter in the soil and as a mulch, and not treating them with chemicals—you can be assured that when you drink in their glorious scents, you're not inhaling a cocktail of toxic chemical residues.

Most flowers for cutting need plenty of sun and fertile, free-draining soil. They can be grown in their own separate bed, or fitted in among other plants, but they shouldn't be planted close to overhanging trees. The most useful flowers to grow for cutting are annuals, biennials, or perennials, but bulbs will provide

Picking tips

● Pick flowers early in the day for a longer vase life.

● Cut the stems with a sharp pair of scissors or pruners—crushing the stems will shorten their vase life.

● Put the flowers in a clean vase with fresh water and refresh after a few days.

● Some flowers, such as gladioli or cleome, make more of an impact as single stems; others are better massed together in a bunch.

Make a simple feed for your growing plants

Comfrey (*Symphytum* x *uplandicum*) makes an excellent organic liquid feed for plants. Wait for a year after planting the comfrey, then cut leaves from April to September. Pile the leaves in a container with a ¼ in (4–6 mm) wide hole or a faucet at the bottom and cover. Drain the liquid (or let it drip into a jar). Use diluted 1:10 with water if the liquid is thin and brown, 1:20 if it is thick and dark, or store in a bottle for up to a year.

Alternatively, fill a 2 gallon bucket with leaves and weigh down with a stone. Add 1 pt (600 ml) of rainwater, cover and leave in a warm spot.

After 3–4 weeks, strain the liquid into a bowl or dip a jug into the bucket. Store in a bottle. Dilute 1 fl oz (25 ml) per 1¾ pt (liter) of rainwater.

excellent blooms in spring, especially scented narcissi, hyacinths and lily of the valley. Regularly picking star performers such as sweet peas and cosmos will encourage them to produce yet more blooms.

Sow sweet peas, cerinthe, and other hardy annuals early because they tolerate the cold. Half-hardy annuals, such as zinnias, cosmos, and antirrhinums, can be sown indoors and planted out once there's no risk of frost. Late-flowering annuals, such as chrysanthemums, can be sown directly in the ground.

Facts on cut flowers

● A survey of 8,000 Colombian flower workers showed that individuals had been exposed to 127 different pesticides. 20% of these are banned or unregistered in the United States.

● Ecuadorian rose producers typically use six fungicides, four insecticides, three nematicides (used to kill nematodes), and several herbicides on their plants.

● 85% of the UK's cut flowers are imported. Carnations and roses grown in Colombia have to travel 5,500 miles (8,850 km) to get to the UK.

Take your pick

Spring
Daffodil
Hellebore
Lily of the valley
Solomon's seal
Tulip

Summer
Acanthus
Achillea
Ageratum
Antirrhinum
Allium
Aster
Ammi
Calendula
Cerinthe
Cleome
Cornflower
Cosmos
Dianthus
Gaura
Gladiolus
Gypsophila

Love-in-a-mist
Peony
Ranunculus
Roses (especially scented varieties)
Salvia
Scabious
Sunflower
Sweet pea
Zinnia

Fall
Chrysanthemum
Dahlia
Eremurus
Helenium
Nerine
Rudbeckia
Teasel

PRESERVE FRUIT

Freezing, a modern form of preservation, is neither ecological nor seasonal, but it's the best way to preserve most fruits. As long as they are frozen properly, many fruits will keep their color, flavor, and vitamins, and make a welcome addition to dishes in the winter months. Freezing and using sugar (in fruit recipes) are the most common ways of preserving a crop, although drying fruits or mixing them with a high concentration of alcohol will also stop their natural decay.

Two simple principles govern the process of freezing: the food must be as fresh as possible; and it should be frozen rapidly. Fast-freezing limits the disruption of a food's cell structure—although no matter how fast and efficiently you freeze food its structure will inevitably break down; a frozen raspberry will never look the same as a fresh one. A freezer should operate at - 0.5° F (-18° C) or below. At this temperature, the bacteria that spoil food cannot grow.

Most fruits freeze well (with the exception of strawberries), but different procedures suit different fruits. Arrange berries on trays in the freezer and, once frozen, transfer the fruit into rigid containers or plastic bags. Peel and core fruit such as apples and pears, then toss the prepared fruit in a little lemon juice to prevent discoloration before you freeze them. Or pack fruit like plums, peaches and apricots in a cold sugar syrup: make the syrup by boiling 1 cup (225 g) of sugar with 2 cups (600 ml) of water for five minutes. Allow the syrup to cool, then pour over the prepared fruit and freeze. Any fruit can also be frozen as a purée, either cooked or raw. Make all freezer packages as airtight as possible, allowing a little extra space for any liquids to expand, and label them with the contents and date. Frozen fruits are especially good in fruit smoothies, but for other uses thaw the fruit to room temperature first.

A variety of fruit preserves can be made by mixing fruit with sugar. Most preserves are made with 1 lb (500 g) of sugar to every 1 lb (500 g) of fruit, and should keep for at least a year. This is a good way to use up a glut of fruit, and anything you make yourself is infinitely better than bought produce. However, the high temperatures used in making preserves and the amount of sugar required make it a less nutritious form of preservation.

The dehydration technique, which slowly dries fruit by extracting all the moisture, enables fruits to be stored without deteriorating, and is one of the healthiest forms of fruit preservation. If you grow your own fruit, you may prefer to buy a dehydrator. Whether rehydrated or used as they are, dried fruits make an excellent snack food.

Fruits can also be preserved in alcohol—cherries in brandy are particularly good. Simply fill a jar with washed, pitted cherries, add a little sugar, and cover with brandy. Shake the jar about once a week. The cherries are ready to eat after three months, and make a lovely end to a celebration meal. Pears are also a good choice of fruit to preserve *(see right)*.

Dried apples

If you don't have a dehydrator, try either of the two methods below for drying apples. Peel, core, and slice the apples into rings, then put them into a bowl of water mixed with a little lemon juice to prevent them from turning brown.

Air-dried Thread the apple rings onto a piece of string and hang the string by an open fireplace until the apple pieces are completely dried out.

In a conventional oven Hang the apple rings on a bamboo stick that measures the width of your oven, or arrange them on a rack. Leave in the oven for about an hour at 49° C/120° F. Then increase the temperature to 60° C/140° F and leave for three to six hours.

Preserved pears

Pick the best pears from your harvest. If you want to peel, halve and core the pears, quickly blanch them afterward in boiling water for two minutes, then put them in cold water.

In a thick-bottomed pan add 1¼ cups of unrefined sugar to 4 cups of water and boil for five minutes. Meanwhile, put the fruit into a large sterilized, heat-resistant jar, leaving a gap of ¾ in (2 cm) below the rim. When the syrup is ready, pour it over the pears until they are completely covered.

Loosely close the jar without sealing it and place it on a wooden trivet in a pan of boiling water. Simmer the jar for up to 30 minutes, or until the pears are cooked. Then seal the jar shut, allow to cool and store in a cool, dry place.

KEEP A FEW GEESE

Keeping geese seems to have gone a little out of fashion, which is perhaps surprising, as they produce delicious free-range eggs and premium organic meat, will largely look after themselves, and are effective burglar alarms.

Geese are considered low-maintenance livestock, needing little additional feeding so long as grass or other grazing is plentiful; they are natural lawn mowers. As long as they have enough space, they'll be happy. Start by buying a goose and a gander; they will form a bond that will last their lifetime. If you want geese for both eggs and meat, buy at least two geese and one gander so that if you slaughter one goose, the other won't be left alone.

Geese have exceptional eyesight and a wide field of vision. Some breeds can be extremely vocal if they observe something or somebody unfamiliar or sense a perceived threat. As a result, they are occasionally used to guard whisky warehouses and even military installations. If you keep geese for security purposes, a highly strung light breed such as the Chinese goose is a good choice. Before buying any geese, it's worth making sure that your neighbors will not object.

Goose eggs

The laying season for geese starts in midwinter and continues until midsummer. A single goose can lay up to 80 eggs a year, which is remarkable given that the eggs weigh 8 oz (200 g) each. Remove the eggs as soon as possible, but be careful, as geese can be protective of their clutch. The eggs should be stored in a cool, draught-free place in clean egg cartons.

Choose your geese

Geese are grouped into three types—light, medium, and heavy breeds—based on their size and weight. You should select a breed according to whether you want it for eggs or meat: in general, the heavier breeds lay fewer eggs, but all of the breeds may be used for meat. The medium and light breeds are the most practical geese to keep.

If you want to breed geese for the table, heavy breeds like the Toulouse and White Embden, which are twice as big as the other breeds, provide an enormous 24 lb (11 kg) or more of meat, while medium breeds, such as the Saddleback and American Buff, tend to weigh about 14–20 lb (6.5–9 kg). Light breeds, such as the Chinese and Pilgrim geese, produce a 10–14 lb (4.5–6.5 kg) table bird; two small birds are often better-tasting than one large goose. Geese take up to 30 weeks to mature.

Signs of good health in a goose

- Dry nostrils.
- Bright eyes with no soreness.
- Clean, shiny feathers.
- Good weight and musculature for age.
- Clean vent (rear-end) feathers with no smell.
- Straight toes and undamaged webs.
- Alert and active bird with no sign of lameness.

Geese are generally hardy, and most ailments are caused by poor husbandry. As with all poultry, intestinal worms must be controlled.

Saddleback
Like the American Buff, an average egg-layer that produces tasty meat. Docile bird that is perfect for a small home flock.

American Buff
An ideal medium breed. Not as good a layer as smaller breeds, but produces tasty meat for roasting. Calm, docile, and well-suited to a small home flock.

Chinese
A light, intelligent breed, either white with an orange knob and bill, or fawn. Lays an impressive 60 eggs a year, and makes a fierce guard.

Pilgrim
A light and practical breed that is ideal for a hobby farm. The male is all white and the female mainly gray. Lays approximately 20 eggs a year.

Getting started

Geese are more self-sufficient than ducks and like to roam freely. They are not fussy birds and, as long as they have fresh water, mixed corn, grit, and a large supply of grass, they need little else. Their main need is to be protected from foxes and vermin at night.

Geese need to be taught where their home is; if your new arrivals are not used to a goose house, keep them penned up in their house with a large outdoor mesh run for a few days to get them accustomed to their new surroundings. If you don't have a fox-proof fence around the field or area where your geese will roam, shut them in their house every night. A laying goose needs to feel that she is safe and dry in her house, so clean out the shed and the run (if you have one) as often as possible, as geese can be messy.

If grass and other grazing is plentiful, your geese won't need extra feeding for long periods of the year. Allow your geese to forage for their own food: 80 percent of their food will come from grass and weeds. If sufficient natural food is not available, provide chopped greens (cabbage leaves, kale, and lettuce) and cereals (whole grains). Make sure that the geese always have mixed grit freely available. To fatten geese quickly for eating, feed them on ground barley and wheat in equal amounts, twice daily, for three weeks. You can also feed up laying geese in midwinter just before they start to lay.

Geese need access to some water, and a clean pond with proper drainage is ideal. However, unlike ducks, a water trough that is deep enough to allow the geese to dip their heads in and bathe (to avoid skin parasites and sore eyes) will be an adequate substitute. In the summer, you should make sure that your geese have plenty of shade, as they are prone to sunstroke.

A goose keeper's kit

1 **Fresh water**

As with all livestock, geese need access to supplies of fresh water. If you don't have a pond and use a water trough instead, make sure that it is deep enough for the geese to dip their heads.

2 **Open pasture**

Geese are grazing animals, so allow them as much open space as you can. If the grass and weeds are plentiful, they will only need a small amount of supplementary feeding. Confining geese in a small area will damage the grass.

3 **Feed trough**

Use a feed trough when you feed your geese whole grains and chopped greens, otherwise the geese will trample and waste their food.

4 **Goose house**

Each goose needs at least 4 sq ft (120 sq cm) of sleeping space in the house, which can be as simple or as elaborate as you like, as long as it protects the birds from predators at night. A shuttered entrance will help to keep the birds securely inside. The floor should always be kept clean and dry.

5 **Informal nest box**

Laying geese are not fussy about where they lay their eggs, as long as they have a dry, secure nest. Fill an old crate with straw and leave it in a sheltered corner.

6 **Upright nest box**

Alternatively, you can stand a nest box on its side, line it with straw, and position it so that it is sheltered from wind, rain, and sun.

MAKE SUMMER FRUIT JAMS

Homemade jams on a breakfast table are a cheerful sight, and a sweet reminder of the delectable tastes of summer fruits. Making jam is a surprisingly straightforward process, and the filled jars make lovely gifts if you cover the sealed lids with circles of pretty fabric.

Making jam at home doesn't require specialist equipment, but it's a good idea to check that you have a suitable pan with a thick base (there's no need for a lid when making jam). If you want to invest in a preserving pan, buy a heavy-gauge pan. Ideally, preserving jars are best for both jams and chutneys, as they have proper lids that seal down, but glass Mason jars with screw-top lids work just as well. Circles of waxed paper placed (wax-side down) over the top of the jam can also provide a seal. Use firm rather than over-ripe fruit, and wash the fruit several times in cold water before you use it.

Testing for the setting point

Spoon a small amount of the boiling jam onto a plate, pop the plate into the fridge, and allow to cool. The jam is ready if the sample forms a skin that is firm enough to wrinkle when you push it with your fingertip. If the sample remains completely fluid, continue to boil the jam for a few minutes, then re-test.

Sterilizing jars & lids

Jars for jams and pickles should always be scrupulously clean. Wash jars well and place in a moderate oven for five minutes to sterilize them.

Blueberry jam

(Makes 5 lb/ 2.2 kg)

Ingredients

2½ lb (1 kg) fresh blueberries, washed

2 cups (570 ml) water

4 lb (2 kg) unrefined sugar

Method

■ Put the fruit and water into a thick-bottomed pan. Simmer gently for 30 minutes. Add a little extra water if needed to stop the mixture from burning.

■ Add the sugar and stir until dissolved. Boil rapidly for 10–15 minutes.

■ Test for the setting point, take the pan off the heat, then spoon into jars and seal.

Variation

Raspberry jam

Use 2½ lb (1 kg) fresh raspberries.

Strawberry jam

(Makes 5 lb/ 2.2 kg)

Ingredients

3 lb (1.3 kg) fresh strawberries

Juice of 2 lemons

3 lb (1.3 kg) unrefined sugar

Method

■ Cook the fruit and juice in a thick-bottomed pan over a low heat until the juices run (10–15 mins).

■ Add the sugar and stir until dissolved. Bring to the boil and cook rapidly for 15 minutes.

■ Test for the setting point, then spoon into jars and seal.

Variation

Strawberry & lime jam

Use the juice of 1 lemon and 2 limes. Add the zest of 2 limes before putting the jam into jars.

GROW PLANTS TO ATTRACT WILDLIFE

If you have some soil, flowering plants and shrubs, a tree or two, and a bird bath or a small pond, then you'll have wildlife in your yard—and probably in much greater quantities than you realize.

Much wildlife will be tiny—some even microscopic—but these creatures form the base of the food chain that feeds the mammals, birds, and amphibians that increasingly rely on yards for their survival; many insects, such as bumblebees and moths, are in decline.

Providing for beneficial insects that pollinate as they travel around the yard, fly from one yard to the next, or feed on pests such as aphids (one hoverfly larva can eat around 1,000 aphids in its lifetime) is one of the most helpful ways to support wildlife. Flowers, for example, provide nectar and pollen, which insects such as butterflies, bees, hoverflies, and lacewings need. Both native and non-native plants can provide this, but they must have flower structures that allow the insects to get at the nectar and pollen.

By providing different areas to feed, shelter, and breed in, and water to drink, you will make your yard an even better refuge for wildlife. You'll be rewarded with the pleasure of watching or hearing these wild creatures feed, drink, and move around.

Try to include as many of the following as you can in your yard or garden:

Trees No matter how small or large, trees provide song posts and shelter for birds. Mature trees can make excellent nest sites for birds such as treecreepers, chickadees, and woodpeckers. Some species, especially native trees, also harbor huge numbers of insects and invertebrates. Willows, for example, are an important plant food for moths which, in turn, attract bats.

Ground cover Many creatures, such as ground beetles and centipedes, need the dark, moist conditions that exist underneath groundcover plants or plant material to survive. Frogs and toads can find shelter under low-growing plants, too.

Shrubs Along with trees, shrubs provide natural windbreaks, creating sheltered areas that are needed by insects such as butterflies and bees. The leaves, flowers, berries, fruit, and seeds of shrubs also provide food for many creatures.

Flowering plants Plan to have plants in flower from early until late in the growing season. Early foragers such as bees, and late feeders such as butterflies, particularly need help. Avoid double flowers, multi-petaled forms, or hybrid cultivars that do not produce pollen or nectar.

Flowers from two families, Apiaceae and Asteraceae, are good to plant: Apiaceae (includes umbellifers such as fennel and dill) produce huge amounts of nectar over a short period of time; Asteraceae (daisylike flowers including asters and sunflowers) produce smaller amounts over a long period.

Climbing plants Climbers provide homes for insects and small mammals, and nest sites for small birds. By growing these plants up bare fences or walls you can, from a wildlife point of view, increase the size of your yard.

Berries & seeds By planting species that bear berries and fruits, and leaving seed-bearing stems standing at the end of the growing season, you will help birds and small mammals survive the winter months when their natural food sources are greatly reduced. Standing stems also provide hibernation sites for insects.

Grass Long grass makes an excellent habitat for insects such as damselflies, grasshoppers, and other small creatures, while birds such as starlings and blackbirds will hunt for invertebrates in grass. Some butterflies also lay their eggs in grasses. If you have a lawn, leave a section of it uncut as a natural habitat for these different creatures.

Hedges Hedges, especially hawthorn, guelder rose, hazel, and beech, create shelter and homes for a wide number of creatures. Hedges also create essential corridors for wildlife to move from one area to another in safety.

Plants that provide early pollen and nectar

■ Trees such as willow *(Salix caprea)*, hazel *(Coryllus avellana)*, mimosa.

■ Shrubs such as *Viburnum tinus*, mahonia, bramble.

■ Bulbs such as crocus, grape hyacinth *(Muscari)*, snowdrop *(Gallanthus)*.

■ Flowers such as Forget-me-not *(Myosotis)*, primrose *(Primula)*, wallflower *(Cheiranthus)*.

Plants that provide late pollen and nectar

■ Shrubs such as *Buddleja*.

■ Flowering plants such as ivy *(Hedera)*, sedum *(Sedum* species), Michaelmas daisy *(Aster* species), coneflower *(Echinacea* species), rudbeckia *(Rudbeckia* species), heather *(Calluna* and *Erica* species), fennel *(Foeniculum vulgare)*.

Other ways that you can make your garden or yard attractive to wildlife

■ Leave a few piles of dead wood on the ground, which will be used by a wide variety of invertebrates, and serve as a shelter for frogs, toads, and newts.

■ Leave out food for birds, especially in the winter and spring.

■ Make a pond with shallow edges, and grow some native plants in and around it.

■ Put up nest boxes for birds, bats and owls.

■ Make nesting sites for solitary bees by drilling holes of different dimensions in wood.

■ Put up homes for overwintering insects, such as ladybugs and lacewings.

Did you know?

● It's good news for plants to have birds eating their berries, as the birds drop or excrete the seeds and so enable the plants to spread. Birds are attracted to bright red yew berries, for example. They swallow the fruit, but then spit out the seed, which has a poisonous (and bad-tasting) coating.

● Fennel *(Foeniculum vulgare)* is a gardener's friend: it can attract around 500 species of insect, more than half of them devourers of pests such as aphids and caterpillars.

● In the UK, the native oak *(Quercus robur)* supports 284 species of insect; the non-native horse chestnut *(Aesculus hippocastanum)* supports just four species.

MAKE BERRY POPSICLES & FRUIT COMPOTE

Soft fruits like berries won't keep for long after they've been picked, so one of the best ways to preserve their heavenly juices and sweet summer taste is to turn them into popsicles or compote, which can also be frozen. The compote is delicious with ice cream, in a pie or as the basis of a summer pudding.

Berry popsicles

Ingredients

1 cup (250 g) finely granulated sugar
1 cup (250 ml) water
1 lb (500 g) fresh berries—either raspberries, strawberries, or blackberries, washed
½ cup (100 ml) fresh lemon juice

Method

■ Make a sugar syrup first: put the sugar and water in a thick-bottomed saucepan. Place the pan over a low heat and stir the mixture with a wooden spoon until the sugar has dissolved.

■ Turn up the heat and bring the syrup to a steady boil for five minutes. Then turn off the

heat and allow the syrup to cool.

■ Purée the berries by passing them through a sieve, which will also remove all the seeds.

■ Mix the berry purée with the lemon juice and sugar syrup. Taste the mixture, and if you think that it needs to be sweeter, stir in a little sifted powdered sugar. If you prefer the taste to be a little sharper, add some more lemon juice.

■ Pour the mixture into popsicle molds, slot an ice cream stick into each mold, and freeze the popsicles until required.

Variation

Rhubarb popsicles

You can also make fruit popsicles using rhubarb, but you need to cook the fruit first.

■ Place 2 lb 4oz (1 kg) of washed fruit in a pan, barely cover the fruit with water, and add 1 cup (250 g) of finely granulated sugar.

■ Stir over a low heat until the sugar has dissolved, then simmer for about five minutes until the fruit is completely tender.

■ Leave to cool for a few minutes, then pour the fruit and juices into a large nylon sieve set over a jug.

■ Push the fruit through the sieve to create a smooth purée.

■ Taste the purée and, if it needs it, stir in a little sifted powdered sugar. Pour into molds, push in the ice cream sticks, and freeze the popsicles until needed.

Forest fruit compote

Ingredients

½ cup (100 g) blackberries
½ cup (100 g) raspberries
½ cup (100 g) finely granulated sugar
A dash of lemon juice

Method

■ Put all the berries in a small bowl, add the sugar, and leave to macerate for at least 1 hour.

■ Add the lemon juice and set aside to be used, or freeze in sealed containers until required.

GROW COMPANION PLANTS

When European monks planted clumps of chives under roses in their walled gardens in medieval times, the term "companion planting" hadn't yet been coined, but they were certainly practicing it: deliberately growing a particular plant because of its effect on another plant. In this case, the chives, probably due to their pungent oils, were thought to keep aphids away from the roses and to keep diseases like blackspot at bay.

Common pests that companion plants will help to repel

Blackfly

Carrot fly

Flea beetles

Greenfly

Leafhoppers

Thrips

Whitefly

Wireworms

Organic gardeners today can make use of lots of companion plants to protect vulnerable crops and to fertilize the soil. Although there is scientific evidence for only some of these practices, it's well worth giving them a try, both in the vegetable bed or garden and in your flower borders, as it helps gardeners understand the natural rhythms of a planted garden. It's also inexpensive—the price of a pack of seeds—if you grow the plants yourself.

There are various ways in which plants can be good companions
Providing shelter and shade In temperate gardens, strong winds can kill off certain plants by buffeting them and chilling the air temperature by as much as 15–20°F (10°C), especially in the winter and early spring when the young plants are beginning to grow new shoots.

The best kind of shelter for vulnerable plants is other plants, such as those suitable for hedging and trees, that will filter the wind, but not block it completely (a solid windbreak creates a

void, which draws down the wind in eddies, creating even worse damage). Other plants, such as deciduous trees, create the shade that woodland species such as ferns need to thrive.

Attracting beneficial insects While there are some insects that attack the plants in the garden, there's an army of other insects that are beneficial, either because they pollinate plants (which is especially useful for certain fruits and vegetables) or they prey on pests such as aphids. Flowering plants with accessible supplies of nectar and pollen—for example, tubular-shaped flowers such as foxgloves for long-tongued butterflies and bumblebees, and flat, open flowers such as asters for ladybugs and lacewings—will provide food for these insects. By making sure that you have a succession of these flowers (they should be single flowers, not doubles or multi-petaled), from early spring onward, you are likely to have a healthy population of helpful insects in your garden or vegetable plot throughout the growing season.

Confusing and repelling pests Certain plants seem to keep pests away from their target plants by confusing them. Pot marigolds (*Calendula*) are useful to plant at the base of vegetables such as tomatoes and cucumbers as they draw whitefly away from the crops, possibly because of their bright petals. In the same way nasturtiums act like a beacon for blackfly and cabbage caterpillars. Mustard *(Brassica hirta)* is a useful plant to grow with potatoes, as wireworms are attracted to its roots. Many insects recognize their food plant by its smell, so growing a strongly aromatic plant such as mint, sage, onion, or parsley close to carrots can confuse the carrot fly so that it doesn't find its preferred plant. French marigolds (*Tagetes*) have a strong smell that seems to keep aphids away. Chives and garlic, which are rich in volatile oils, also seem to repel insects such as leafhoppers and aphids.

Providing nutrients Certain plants benefit others by making nutrients accessible to them. Beans and other legumes convert nitrogen gas from the air into a form they can use in their roots, and when they die this valuable nutrient is released into the soil. Comfrey and borage provide extra potassium and calcium for neighboring plants, while parsley seems to make tomatoes more vigorous and asparagus helps potato plants to grow strong.

Super companions

1 Calendula *(C. officinallis)*
Provides nectar and pollen for insects until late fall and attracts whitefly and other pests.

2 Candytuft *(Iberis umbellata)*
Long-flowering annual that provides nectar and pollen for insects and, if planted under brassicas, reduces flea beetles.

3 Onion *(Allium cepa)*
Interplanted with carrots, it may help to reduce carrot fly and thrips.

4 Marigold *(Tagetes)*
Its strong smell may help to repel aphids such as greenfly and blackfly.

5 Yarrow *(Achillea millefolium)*
Attracts predatory wasps, ladybugs, and hoverflies, and can improve vigor in neighboring plants.

6 Nasturtium *(N. officinale)*
Helps to deflect aphids from broccoli and squash and acts as a decoy near cabbages.

7 Chives *(Allium schoenoprasum)*
Attracts beneficial insects and may repel aphids from plants.

8 Garlic *(Allium sativum)*
Can confuse pests such as leafhoppers, aphids, and carrot fly.

9 Poached egg plant *(Limnanthes douglasii)*
Long-flowering annual that provides nectar and pollen for insects.

KEEP HONEY BEES

Bees exist in almost every part of the world, and are one of the most useful of all insects—not only is their honey highly prized and their beeswax useful, they also play a crucial role in pollinating plants, encouraging flowers to bloom for longer, and generating richer crops of fruit and vegetables.

There are about 20,000 species of bees, but it is only honey bees that make honey and wax in large amounts. Honey bees (workers, drones, and queens) are fascinating creatures: they have their own social system and complex behavioral patterns, which we are only just beginning to understand. Working with a community of bees offers an absorbing and unique insight into the annual cycles and workings of the natural world.

The beekeeper's calendar

Before you start keeping bees, it's important to understand the annual life cycle of bees and the tasks you will need to perform as a beekeeper.

Early spring The queen bee starts to lay eggs in February. The honey stores in the hive will be running low after the winter because—despite the emergence of spring flowers—nectar and pollen are in very short supply. Fill the bees' feeder with sugar syrup, if necessary, to supplement the natural nectar around.

Late spring There's a rapid increase in the brood. The bees fly on fine warm days to gather nectar and pollen from the early blossoms. This is the time to make the removable "supers" (frames inside the hive that contain chambers where the honey is stored), and fix in place the queen excluder, which prevents the queen from laying eggs in the honey store.

Summer Pollen and nectar are in abundant supply for the bees. This is the busiest season for a beekeeper, as the hive needs to be checked weekly and boxes of supers added and removed as necessary. The main skill of beekeeping is to prevent "swarming"—when a new queen leaves the hive, taking possibly more than half of the colony's bees with her. This happens when the bees detect that the hive is becoming too cramped and cells for new queens form. These cells are long and pointed compared to normal cells, and are often hidden in corners and difficult to find. Any queen cups (empty cells built in preparation for queen larvae) and cells you find should be destroyed by squashing them with a hive tool. By late summer the supers are full of honey; watch out for wasps trying to rob the hive.

Fall The bees are past swarming by this time, and the beekeeper can begin to relax and harvest the honey. Once you have removed the honey store and effectively taken away the bees' winter food store, feed them with sugar syrup. It's also important to protect your hive from the Varroa mite, which carries a virus: remove the supers and suspend two medicated plastic strips in the brood frame. The strips contain chemicals that are slowly released into the hive and kill the mites. Remove the strips after six weeks; if you do detect an infection, treatment is possible, so seek professional advice.

Winter After collecting the last of the fall nectar, the bees remain in the hive. The drones are expelled from the hive to die in the cold, as they are no longer useful and the honey store is needed for the queen and the workers. The bees collect in a mass in the center of the hive, close to their food supply. Once the bees have shut up shop for the winter, don't disturb them.

Buy your bees

Spring is the time to acquire your bees. Your local beekeeping organization or group will be happy to give advice and supply you with the equipment and bees: it's best to purchase a "nucleus" of bees (a queen and worker bees) from an experienced beekeeper or specialist supplier. The colony will have a frame containing a single queen, worker bees, cells of eggs, and developing grubs. The queen is larger than the workers, with a more pointed rear end. She does have a sting, but will only use it on a rival queen. To identify the queen, carefully mark a colored dot, using a marker, on her head.

Place the queen in a small plastic container in the brood chamber (where she lays her eggs in the frames) and seal the container with a hard candy. The worker bees become accustomed to the queen's smell in the time that it takes them to eat the candy. They will then accept her and she will start to lay eggs. Feed the new colony with sugar syrup for the first week until they build up their own honey store.

Getting started

There are different types of hive to choose from. Some are made of wood, others are made of plastic. To avoid disease, it's best to begin with a new hive, but secondhand hives can be used, provided that they are thoroughly cleaned and repaired where necessary. If you purchase a new hive, you'll need to make your own frames, and repair and maintain the hive later on, so it's important to have a basic understanding of woodwork skills. The hive should be located in a warm, sheltered position facing south, away from overhanging trees. The bees prefer to have a clear flight path into and out of the hive, as they enter and leave at approximately a 60-degree angle. To prevent the base of the hive from rotting, and for ease of access, build a brick platform on which to stand the hive.

Making a frame from a kit

Don't use secondhand frames—they can carry disease. Save money by making your own frames, or use kits: the precut ends should slot easily together.

Slot the thin wax sheet of foundation, which is stamped with a hexagonal pattern that acts as a guide for the bees to construct their honey, into the sides of the frame.

Hammer in the pins to fix the lower edge of the frame. The fixing needs to be firm or the frame will come apart when heavily laden with the bees' honey.

Your hive should always be well maintained and cared for. A broken hive will be harder to disassemble smoothly (and will upset the bees), and may allow "robbers," such as wasps and other bees, to find their way in and steal honey. It can even result in your bees moving out of their home.

A new colony won't produce a significant yield of honey in its first year, but an established hive can produce up to 60 lb (27 kg) of honey in a good year. The type of honey produced depends on the availability of flowers and foliage in the area (clear honey, for example, is produced by bees collecting nectar from garden flowers). It's possible to produce speciality honey, such as heather, clover, or orange blossom, from a single source of nectar by placing the hive out of range of all other nectar sources. This can be difficult to achieve, so if you are new to beekeeping, a blended honey may be the best option.

A beekeeper's kit

You can purchase a hive, suit, tools, and honey extractor from specialist suppliers or through your local beekeeping organization. Keep all your equipment in good condition.

Clothing
- A good-quality bee suit, helmet, and veil.
- Long rubber or leather gloves and boots. Ideally, all clothing should be white, a color that bees find soothing.

Smoker & other tools
- Use a smoker before opening the hive: after three minutes, the bees become drowsy and fill their sacks with honey, believing that there is a nearby fire and danger is ahead. With full honey sacks, it's then hard for them to use their stings. Burn dry hay or grass cuttings to produce the smoke (or some beekeepers use strips of burlap, as it burns for longer).
- A soft brush to gently remove the bees from the honey frames.
- A feeder to supplement the bees' diet with sugar syrup.
- A hive tool, a flat piece of metal with a curved end, to open the hive and to loosen supers that have become stuck together.

Harvesting honey

Part the bees from their honey by placing an "extra crown board," fitted with a bee escape, between the brood box and the super (where the honey is). This allows the bees to go into the brood chamber (where the queen lays her eggs), but not to return to the super. Allow at least 24 hours to clear a hive; by the next day, the majority of your bees will be safe in the brood chamber.

Smoke the hive and remove the roof and crown board underneath. Remove the supers to a safe place where the bees can't access them. A hive will need 20–30 lb (10–14 kg) of honey to survive the winter, so don't take all the harvest. Slow, deliberate movements won't disturb the bees as much as quick movements will (bees can sense uncertainty or panic and won't respond positively). You can estimate how much honey there is as you lift each frame; if it doesn't weigh much, it's better left for the bees. Lightly brush off any bees down into the hive.

Slice off the workers bees' wax caps (which seal the honey inside the cells) with a warmed knife.

Place the supers in a honey extractor, a centrifugal separator that throws the honey off the frames.

Strain the honey through a honey strainer for 24 hours, then decant into clean, sterilized jars and seal.

The beeswax can be used in candles, polishes, and other products. The empty frames can be left out by the hive for the bees to clean up.

CHOOSE A GREEN CHRISTMAS TREE

For many of us, an intrinsic part of our Christmas celebrations involves putting up and decorating a conifer tree, and enjoying the resiny smell of its needles and the cheerful sight of the decorated branches for several weeks in the middle of winter. Although we are beginning to understand the importance of recycling our cut trees—they can be reduced to chippings and put back into the environment as mulch and in soil improvers—a vast number of Christmas trees are still sent to landfill sites.

There are two ways of making your Christmas tree as "green" as possible: either buy a living tree, and after Christmas plant it in the yard as an ornamental tree or keep it in its pot outside to get a second chance of using it the following Christmas; or buy a cut tree that has been grown sustainably (look for a Christmas tree growers' association label or logo)—preferably from a local grower to minimize transportation miles—and ensure that the tree is recycled after you've used it. Many cities arrange special recycling facilities for trees after Christmas, and some growers will take back and recycle any tree purchased from them.

Some Christmas tree conifers can grow to great heights—the Nordmann fir *(Abies nordmanniana)* can reach 131 ft (40 m)—so if you plan to plant yours outside, check on its eventual height first. Any container-grown conifer will look suitably Christmassy and, if you buy a dwarf conifer, you should be able to keep it in a pot for several years if you feed, water, and re-pot it regularly. Many Christmas tree growers offer more unusual varieties, such as the Colorado Blue spruce *(Picea pungens* "Glauca"*)*, which grows to 80 ft (24 m), or the Korean Fir *(Abies koreana)*, which has purple cones and grows to 30 ft (10 m).

How to take care of a living tree

● Buy a container-grown tree, at a maximum height of about 5 ft (1.5 m), and soak it well before bringing it into the house.

● Keep the tree away from direct heat, such as radiators or open fireplaces, and water regularly, just as for most house plants.

● Don't keep the tree indoors for more than a month, as the warmth and artificial lights of your home can make the tree break dormancy and start to put on new growth. Putting the tree outside at that point could kill it.

● After Christmas, take the tree outdoors. Either transplant it in early spring into a larger container (use a bark-based coarse organic compost with some slow-release organic fertilizer, and keep it well watered) or plant it into the ground in well-drained soil that's not frosted. Make the planting hole a generous size, add some bonemeal, and keep the tree well watered for the first couple of years.

DESIGN A HERB GARDEN

Herbs were among the earliest plants grown, mainly for their medicinal uses, by gardeners. Today they are still really satisfying plants to grow. They don't take up much room, so you can grow many different kinds in a small space, and they can provide you with year-round fresh leaves for the kitchen and home remedies. Many of them are wonderfully aromatic, and have striking foliage and flowers. Growing herbs organically will also ensure that any you pick will be free from harmful chemicals.

You can grow herbs in a variety of ways: in gaps in gravel or between stepping stones; in a collection of individual pots; grouped together in a ceramic sink; among the other flowering plants in beds or borders; as edging along paths; or in their own designated beds. The size, location and style of your garden will to some extent dictate how you grow herbs, but the first thing you need to decide is what you want to grow your herbs for.

Ask yourself:
- Do you mainly want to use herbs in the kitchen and in remedies?
- Do you want them to provide a sensory part of the garden, full of scent and attracting pollinating insects such as bees?
- To create a decorative feature, such as a grid of equal-sized beds divided by crisp gravel paths, edged with tiles or wood, and filled with a counterpane of green, gray, purple, yellow, and silver foliage?
- Or maybe you want an all-purpose herb area, which gives you elements of all these things?

Next, consider some practicalities:

Eventual height and spread Check how big the plants will eventually grow, so that you can be sure they will fit in the space allocated. Think about including a mixture of evergreens and annuals, and tall and low plants. Containing the beds in some way—whether with clipped plants or hard materials—will make them easier to manage.

Growing conditions Many herbs originally grew wild in the Mediterranean, and so prefer dry, well-drained sunny sites— although some, such as parsley and mint, do better if shaded from the midday sun. Herbs such as basil are tender annuals, while mint and rosemary are hardy evergreens.

Choice of herbs What will you enjoy looking at or cooking with?

Site If you want to cook with herbs, try to position them close to the kitchen door; if you want to make a feature, choose a spot where the herbs will not be obscured by a more dominant feature. A bed of up to 4 ft (1.2 m) wide will allow you to care for the plants and pick their leaves from the path.

Herb beds

Traditionally, herbs were grown in a number of rectangular beds, with paths in between, but they grow well in beds of various shapes—from "wheels" divided into equal sections, each planted with a single variety, to ovals, ellipses, triangles, and squares. Visit gardens with herb areas for inspiration, then draw up your plan.

Formal designs These are often geometric and edged with tightly clipped plants. They often make use of repeat plantings of evergreens, such as cotton lavender, thyme, hyssop, or hedge germander, to make strong, symmetrical patterns. These herb gardens are high maintenance, as they need regular clipping and very precise planting.

Semi-formal designs Usually make use of clipped box edgings filled with looser plantings of herbaceous herbs.

Informal designs Appear loose and unplanned, but need to be worked out before planting so that there's a balance of large and smaller species, and an attractive mix of colors.

Herbs for the kitchen

Basil *(Ocimum)*

Bay *(Laurus nobilis)*

Chives *(Allium schoenoprasum)*

Dill *(Anethum graveolens)*

Fennel *(Foeniculum vulgare)*

French tarragon *(Artemisia dracunculus)*

Oregano *(Origanum vulgare)*

Mint *(Mentha)*

Parsley *(Petroselinum crispum)*

Rosemary *(Rosmarinus officinalis)*

Sage *(Salvia officinalis)*

Salad burnet *(Sanguisorba minor)*

Sweet marjoram *(Origanum majorana)*

Thyme *(Thymus vulgaris)*

Winter savory *(Satureja montana)*

Aromatic herbs

Basil *(Ocimum)*

Catnip *(Nepeta)*

Coriander *(Coriandrum sativum)*

Cotton lavender *(Santolina)*

Curry plant *(Helichrysum italicum)*

Lavender *(Lavandula* species*)*

Lemon balm *(Melissa officinalis)*

Lemon verbena *(Aloysia triphylla)*

Sage *(Salvia officinalis)*

Wild oregano *(Origanum vulgare)*

Decorative herbs

Alchemilla *(Alchemilla mollis)*

Bergamot *(Monarda fistulosa)*

Borage *(Borago officinalis)*

Blue Hyssop *(Hyssopus officinalis)*

Cardoon *(Cynara cardunculus)*

Chives *(Allium schoenoprasum)*

Curry plant *(Helichrysum angustifolium)*

Dill *(Anethum graveolens)*

Cone flower *(Echinacea* species*)*

Fennel *(Foeniculum vulgare)*

Lavender *(Lavandula* species*)*

Rue *(Ruta graveolens)*

Sage *(Salvia officinalis)*

Yarrow *(Achillea millefolium)*

Growing tips

All herbs need well-drained soil. To improve the structure of the soil, add bulky organic material such as garden compost, well-rotted manure, or leafmold in the spring once you've cleared any weeds.

■ Spread a mulch, such as leafmold or bark, which are low in nutrients and suit herbs well. This helps to retain moisture, suppress weeds, and improve the condition of the soil.

■ In the summer, lightly cut back herbs after flowering and feed them to encourage a second flush of leaves.

■ In the fall, dig in well-rotted manure or garden compost around established plants, but be careful not to touch their stems.

■ In the winter, protect tender herbs with plastic during cold snaps.

■ Raised beds are a good idea if your soil is unsatisfactory, or you want to make a feature of your herbs. When making a raised bed on top of soil, add a good layer of rubble followed by gravel and then at least 1½ in (4 cm) of topsoil mixed with grit or bark (three parts topsoil to one part grit or bark). The retaining walls should be 12–30 in (30–75 cm) high and made from sturdy materials such as logs, sleepers, or bricks.

■ Don't plant dill and fennel together, as they cross-pollinate.

■ Control the roots of mint by either growing the plant in a large pot sunk in the ground, or containing it in the soil with a "box" made of slabs or tiles.

HARVEST & STORE ORCHARD FRUITS

The secret of successful harvesting is to know when to pick particular fruit. Some crops are best picked before they turn ripe; others, such as stone fruits, should be tree-ripened if you want the best flavor. Trees that have been grown in optimum conditions produce the best crops for storage; immature crops, or those that have received too little water and nutrients or suffered from pest and disease damage, won't store well. There are a few simple golden rules to follow when harvesting and storing orchard fruits to help preserve them for several months.

■ Fruit should always be harvested when it reaches optimum maturity—when the fruit is the best quality. If a fruit is very ripe, it will soon start to deteriorate if it's not eaten.

■ Pick hard fruits such as apples and pears when they are just under-ripe, as they will continue to ripen once they have been picked. Fruit growing on the sunniest side of the tree will ripen first.

■ Careful handling is essential, as fruit can be easily bruised. Orchard fruits should be harvested by twisting and lifting the fruit up, not by pulling straight down, and placing it gently—not dropping it—into your harvesting containers. Apples and pears should be picked by holding the fruit with the palm of the hand and avoiding finger pressure. Leave the stalks intact.

■ Only pick fruit (this also applies to soft fruit) on a dry day, as any moisture will encourage mold. If it has rained the night before, wait a day or two before harvesting.

Tips on storing apples

● The ideal temperature for storing apples is 36–41°F (2–5°C).

● Medium-sized apples will store better than very small or very large apples.

● Store apples that ripen at different times separately. Earlier cultivars will speed up the maturity of later ones if they are stored together.

● Early-season varieties do not store well, and are best eaten quickly after harvesting, or cooked into a purée and stored in the freezer.

● Crops from mid-season cultivars can last well for four to five weeks if stored in the right conditions.

● Late-season varieties, which ripen in late September, can be stored for up to eight months. These fruits won't develop their full flavor until they have been stored for some time.

Storing fruits

Select only the best fruits for storing; any fruit that is bruised, has broken skin or shows signs of pest or disease damage should not be stored. The storeroom must be frost-free, safe from pests, rainproof, and ideally at a constant temperature with air circulating freely so that the atmosphere doesn't get too dry or hot and humid. Different crops have different temperature and humidity requirements, but a suitable average temperature is 40–50°F/4–7°C. A cool, dark outdoor storeroom or cellar is ideal; a garden shed or garage may need extra insulation in severe weather; basements and unheated rooms are also suitable; and attics are best avoided due to fluctuations in temperature and humidity.

■ Discard any fruit with bruises, blemishes, or skin punctures, which will soon cause the fruit to rot.

■ Store the fruits slightly apart from each other in a single layer on slatted shelves, fruit trays, or in boxes in a cool, dark place. Apples benefit from being wrapped individually in newspaper, or wax paper for prolonged life.

■ Cover the shelves or boxes with fine chicken wire to prevent pests from nibbling the fruit.

■ Check your stored crops regularly—preferably weekly— and remove any fruits that are turning moldy.

■ Pears are at their best for a short time only. Inspect them frequently, and bring them into a warm room when they are nearly ripe to finish off the process.

Storing citrus fruits

Lemons and other citrus fruits can be wrapped and stored much like apples, or you can keep them in boxes of sand. Put layers of unblemished fruits into wooden crates or paper-lined boxes and cover each layer with dry sand. The fruit should keep for up to two months in this way.

KEEP A MILKING COW

If you have the room and the commitment, a cow is a great addition to a hobby farm. In return for grass, supplementary food in the winter, and good care, she will provide you with milk, cheese, and butter.

Cows are hardy animals that can give a good return on your investment by providing many useful and saleable products, but they do require a high level of commitment. If you want to keep a cow for a near-constant supply of milk, then you will need to milk her twice a day, every day, and get involved in calving—a cow cannot produce her milk without newborn calves. So be prepared for the time involved: either you or someone else will always need to do the milking.

Signs of good health in a cow

- A shiny coat, with a gleam or "bloom" in the hairs.
- Bright eyes.
- A moist muzzle, and a clean (not runny) nose.
- Sweet breath.
- Soft, pliable udders free from lumps.

If a cow is healthy, her milk supply will depend on how well she is fed and kept.

Choose your cow

The main breeds of cow that will interest a hobby farmer are those that produce good quantities of high-quality milk, as well as good beef calves. The best approach is to purchase a three- to four-year-old "in calf" (pregnant) cow that has already calved. She should also have been tested for tuberculosis. Your cow will have a useful, productive life of about 12 years.

Holstein Fresian
Large black and white cow. The breed is most commonly used in large-scale farming, as it is an excellent provider of milk. Because of its temperament and size, it needs skillful handling.

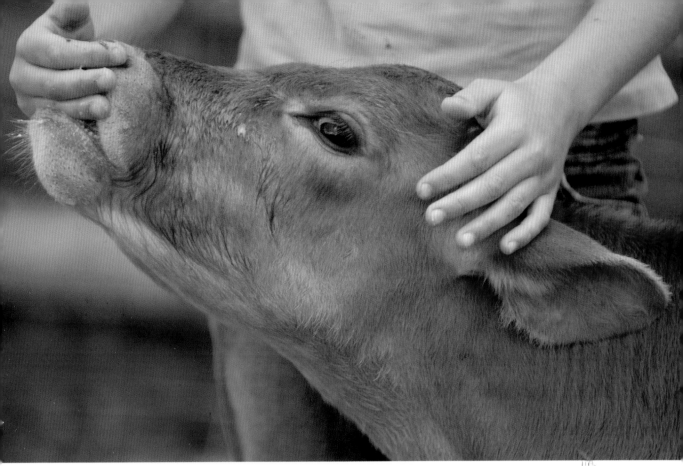

Jersey or Guernsey
These breeds provide very rich, good quality milk and have
the advantage of being attractive, adaptable, and docile animals.
They are suited to a wide range of climates. Easily handled
and milked.

Red Poll
An old breed, the Red Poll is a useful animal for milk and meat.
It is very hardy and thrives outside. Naturally hornless.
Easy to handle and a good feeder.

Caring for your cow

A cow is naturally a grazing animal, so she should be kept outdoors except in times of extreme weather—very cold and wet, or very hot. The precise conditions your cow will be able to withstand will depend on the breed, as some breeds are hardier than others, but a shed is a basic requirement. It must have straw bedding and be cleaned out daily when in use. All gates and fencing to your paddock must be strong. If you have a cow and a calf, you will need a good grazing meadow of at least five acres (two hectares) and access to water. If your cow has been transported by road to her new home, she will be stressed after her trip, so give her lots to drink and a good feed.

Feeding through the year

Grass is the best food for cows, and rich pasture results in rich milk. Your cow will get what she needs nutritionally from the grass during the summer, but in the winter, she will need supplementary feed in the form of roughage—straw or hay—and cereals for protein and carbohydrates, along with other foodstuffs such as kale or beets.

You will also need to provide what is called a "maintenance ration" for your cow—that is, what she needs for her own purposes—as well as a "production ration," which will help her to provide enough milk for your needs. It is best to ask your local hobby farm or family farming groups for advice on the recommended quantities of feed for your breed and climate, but as a guide, you should provide 12–20 lb (5.5–9 kg) of hay as a maintenance ration

Basic equipment

1 Winter feed
Cows will nibble at grass in the winter, but its nutritional value is very low at this time, so they need to eat hay, cereal feed such as rolled oats or barley, and root vegetables such as beets grown for livestock.

2 Salt lick
Mineral deficiencies can be fatal. Provide a block of salt and let your cow judge when and whether she needs it.

3 Hay
Hay provides the required roughage in your cow's diet during the winter. It's worth making your own hay during the summer months.

4 Calf creep feeder
A durable creep feeder allows easy access to additional feed for small to medium-sized calves while they are still suckling the cow.

5 Pasture
Your cow will need good summer pasture from spring to fall in order to give you enough high-quality milk.

6 Straw for bedding
During the winter, when your cow spends more time in her shed, she should have enough straw for deep bedding and to keep out draughts.

7 Fencing
Spend a few moments every day checking that the fences enclosing your pasture are secure.

You should also get to know a good vet, who is experienced in dealing with livestock, in case your cow contracts illness and diseases such as worms, mastitis, pneumonia, and scours.

Milking a cow

You must milk your cow every 12 hours, every day. Ask an experienced farm hand to show you how to milk a cow.

You can milk your cow outdoors, but it is better to milk her somewhere dry and clean. Provide an area in a shed that can be thoroughly washed down.

Distract your cow with a bucket of feed while you milk her—there's no real need to tie her up. Milking should be a predictable experience for the cow, as it will help to reassure and calm her. Sit on a stool at a right angle to the animal, always on the same side, and lean your head against her. This will be soothing for her, and you can feel if she's about to kick.

Use warm water to carefully clean the cow's udder. Take hold of the teat firmly, sealing the top with your thumb and index finger. Squeeze firmly downward, closing your upper fingers first, to force the milk out. Let the teat go, allowing it to refill with milk. Then repeat the process. Be firm and confident as you milk, or the cow will be detect hesitancy.

during the winter. It's a good idea to supplement the hay and balance your cow's diet by substituting half of the hay with other foods such as kale, mangels, beets, or cabbage in the right quantities. This also helps to extend your supplies of precious and expensive hay. Again, experienced farmers will be able to advise you on how much to feed your cow. It's also a good idea to supplement your cow's diet with vitamins and minerals such as magnesium and calcium.

Cows drink prodigious amounts of water—up to 20 gallons (90 liters) each day—so make sure that you provide plenty of it. You should also provide what is called a "salt lick"—a block of salt in a bucket for your cow to eat as and when she sees fit.

Breeding

The time will come when your cow will need to produce a calf if you want her to keep producing milk. If she has already given birth, she should be "dried off" (when milking stops) 50 days before calving again. You can either introduce your cow to a bull, or have her artificially inseminated by a technician. You should be able to locate the services of a bull through local farming contacts, but it's worth bearing in mind that the size of the bull should match the size of your cow so that she doesn't struggle to carry the resulting calf.

Your cow can be inseminated when she is "in season," or ready to mate. She can indicate this by making loud noises and sometimes, but not always, discharging a mucus. Also, if she is kept with other cows, they will mount her when she is in heat. Being in season will happen at intervals, so if you choose a time in July, for example, to mate your cow, the calf will then be born in April when the grass is growing most strongly. The calf will be born nine months and seven days after your cow has been inseminated.

Feed your cow extra rations of cereal during the last eight weeks of her pregnancy: increase her feed gradually by 2 lb (1 kg) of oats per day, up to 8 lb (3.5 kg) per day until she gives birth.

If the weather is warm and her field is sheltered, your cow will prefer to calve in the open rather than in an unfamiliar barn. Her udder will fill and the muscles in her hind quarters will slacken noticeably, warning you that the birth is imminent. Cows tend to be able to give birth without interference. The calf should be born with its two front feet pointing forward, with its head in between them. If you see that the calf is emerging in any other posture, you will need the help of a vet. If the newborn calf is able to cough and breathe, then just leave it to its mother, who will lick her calf with her rough tongue to clean it. She will also provide colostrum, a thick, yellow kind of milk, for the first few days after the calf's birth. After a day or so, when the calf is strong enough, disinfect its umbilical cord with iodine.

Weaning a calf

As you are keeping a cow for her milk, you may not want to wait for the calf to wean itself in 12 weeks' time, so you can force the issue by taking the calf away from its mother—gradually, at first, for a few hours at a time—when it is a week old. Check that the calf can drink diluted milk from a bucket, then lead it a few steps away from its mother where the animals can still see each other. Feed the calf hay as soon as it can eat, and by the fall, it can be turned into beef or kept for future milking, depending on its gender.

MAKE FRESHLY CHURNED BUTTER

Churning butter used to be a laborious and time-consuming process, but now that we have food processors to do all the hard work in a matter of moments, fresh, deliciously creamy butter is a quick and easy option.

Use fresh heavy cream, ideally at room temperature (about 60°F/15°C), for a sweet cream butter. If you want a more subtle continental flavor, culture the cream first before churning: add two tablespoons of plain yogurt, sour cream, or crème fraîche to 17 fl oz (500 ml) of fresh heavy cream. Leave the cream for 24 hours at a warm room temperature (about 75°F/24°C) and then cool it back down to 60°F (15°C) to make the butter. A digital food thermometer is a useful way of enabling you to control the temperature correctly without having to rely on guesswork.

- To make about 10 oz (300 g) of butter, measure 2 cups (500 ml) of fresh heavy cream. The cream should be at room temperature.
- Fit the normal chopping blade to a food processor or a mixer and whip the cream—it will turn quickly from frothy to thick cream. The cream will stiffen more before separating into thick, pale butterfat and buttermilk.
- Drain off the buttermilk (you can reserve it for making soda bread, or to drink).
- The remaining butterfat should be fluffy and ready to use as butter.

The butter will keep for longer if it's washed and worked at this point, which is an equally simple process: to wash it, add a cupful of iced water to the butterfat in the processor bowl and mix the contents briefly. Pour off the milky water and repeat the process several times until the water remains clear after being mixed with the butterfat. Then decant the butter into a bowl and use a potato masher or a couple of forks to press out the last of the liquid. If you wish, salt the butter to your taste and then roll it into a ball or a pat, or press it into ramekins, and chill in the fridge. The butter should keep for a week or more.

MAKE ORGANIC DRINKS

It's always more pleasurable and satisfying to eat or drink something that you've grown or made yourself. Homemade drinks are a delicious way of enjoying a plentiful crop of fruits, or making something special and a little different for yourself or for guests. Bottled drinks that keep also make great gifts. Use seasonal produce to get the best quality and flavors.

Damson wine

Damson wine is one of the easiest and most successful of homemade wines to make. You will need some home brewing equipment:

A large plastic bucket

A one-gallon glass demijohn for the fermentation, plus an airlock to prevent air from entering the vessel while permitting the carbon dioxide gas produced by alcohol fermentation to escape.

A siphoning tube made of flexible plastic tubing attached to a few feet of hard plastic tubing. The hard tube goes into the demijohn to a point just above the sediment, and a quick suck on the soft end starts the movement of the clear liquid out of the demijohn.

Ingredients

3 lb (1.4 kg) ripe damsons, washed
6 pints water, plus ½ pint water
1 packet commercial wine yeast
3 lb (1.4 kg) unrefined organic sugar

Method

■ Put the damsons in a large, stainless steel pan, cover with the water, and bring to the boil.

■ Allow to cool, then tip into a large bucket, cover with a cloth, and leave overnight.

■ The following day, remove a little of the damson liquid, dissolve the yeast in it, and leave for a few minutes until it appears bubbly. Then add it to the damsons, stir well with a wooden spoon, and cover. Allow to ferment for three days, stirring well three times a day.

■ Gently dissolve the sugar in about ½ pint of water until it forms a clear syrup. Allow to cool, then stir into the damson mixture. Ferment for five days, stirring often.

■ Once the vigorous fermentation stops, strain the mixture and transfer it to a demijohn. Fit with an airlock and store at room temperature for about three months.

■ When the fermentation stops, remove the airlock and syphon into bottles, cork, and leave for six months before drinking.

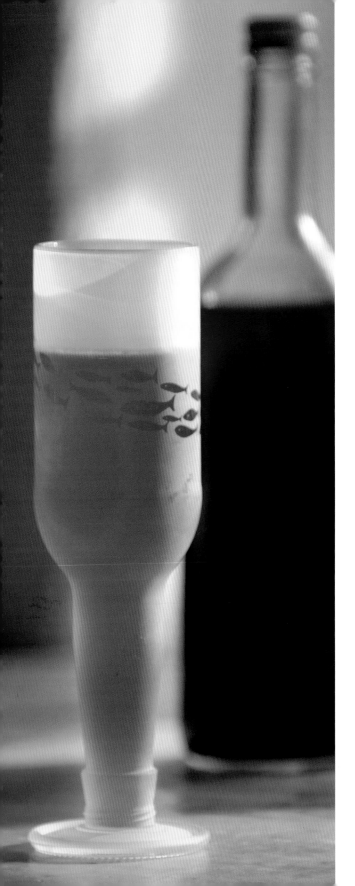

Spiced sloe gin

Ingredients

2 lb (900 g) sloes (blackthorn plums)

2 tablespoons (25 g) honey

Zest of 1 orange

Zest of 1 lemon

1 in (2.5 cm) cube fresh root ginger, thinly sliced

1 cinnamon stick

6 cloves

1 bottle of gin

Method

■ Lightly crush the sloes with the end of a wooden rolling pin.

■ Place in a wide-mouthed bottle and add the honey, orange and lemon zest, ginger, cinnamon stick, and cloves.

■ Fill to the top with gin. Cork and leave in the pantry for between 6–12 months.

Served with sparkling water, sloe gin makes a refreshing drink. Served neat, it makes a good aperitif or after-dinner drink.

Mint lemonade

Ingredients

½ cup (110 g) fresh mint leaves

Juice of 3 lemons

½ cup (110 g) sugar

3 cups (700 ml) water

Method

■ Blend the mint leaves, lemon juice, and sugar together in a processor, then add the water.

■ Pour into a jug and chill well before serving.

Irish coffee

Ingredients

3 tablespoons (44 ml) Irish whiskey

1 teaspoon brown sugar

½ cup (180 ml) strong filter coffee

Heavy cream to taste

Method

■ Combine whiskey, sugar, and coffee together in a mug or a glass. Stir well.

■ Place the tip of a dessert spoon into the coffee at an angle. Gently pour the cream over the spoon so it floats on top of the coffee, and serve.

Apple cider lambs wool

Ingredients

4 sweet or tart apples, peeled and cored

4 cups (1.2 liters) cider

½ cup (125 g) fresh orange juice

8 whole allspice berries

1 in (2.5 cm) cube fresh root ginger, sliced

½ teaspoon nutmeg, freshly grated

½ cup (125 ml) brandy

Method

■ Roast the apples in a moderate oven until soft and pulpy.

■ Heat the remaining ingredients in a stainless steel pan (do not boil). Allow the spices to infuse for ten minutes, then scoop them out.

■ Stir in the apple pulp and serve.

Mulled wine

Ingredients

4 cloves

½ cinnamon stick

A few slices of fresh root ginger

Finely pared peel of 1 lemon

Finely pared peel of 1 orange

1 bottle red wine

1 tablespoon honey

A splash of brandy (optional)

Method

■ Put the spices, peel, and wine in a pan. Heat to just below boiling point. Turn off the heat.

■ Leave to infuse for 1 hour. Then add the honey and brandy, gently reheat and serve.

KEEP A FLOCK OF DUCKS

Ducks are easy and versatile birds to keep, and although they can be noisy, they also have an easy-going, cheerful demeanor. Depending on the breed, they can be a good source of meat, or produce up to 300 eggs each a year.

One of the attractions of keeping ducks is that they don't need elaborate housing—a simple duck house in your yard (or with a large run attached) will suit them well, as long as they have access to plenty of water. They will quickly rid your garden of slugs and snails, their droppings provide a good source of fertilizer, and their used bedding can be added to other yard waste to produce organic compost. Ducks are gregarious birds and respond well to human conversation, becoming calmer and tamer as they get to know your voice.

Getting started

Ducks have few requirements, but it's important that they are happy and contented in their environment, and not overcrowded. You'll need a sufficiently large, securely enclosed area of grass (15 sq yds/12.5 sq m per bird) to allow for a variety of foraging material, and with lots of shady areas, as ducks don't like bright sunlight. Keep the birds away from ornamental gardens and vegetable plots, as they may destroy them. Ideally, your ducks should have clean running water to swim in—or, at the very least, enough clean water for them to immerse their heads and dabble. Dry, clean, predator- and draught-proof housing is also essential, as ducks need somewhere secure to roost overnight to protect them from vermin and foxes. They are sensitive creatures and don't like change, so try to keep their environment constant. They'll be upset by an object lying around, such as a shovel, for example, and will try to avoid it, leading to stress.

Choose your ducks

There isn't a great choice of dual-purpose duck breeds that provide both eggs and meat, so you may decide to keep ducks either for the table or to lay eggs. Four to six ducks and a male, or drake, will be enough to establish a flock for meat, while four or five ducks should provide you with a good supply of eggs (you won't need a drake).

Signs of good health in a duck

- Dry nostrils.
- Bright eyes with no soreness.
- Clean, shiny feathers.
- Good weight and musculature for age.
- Clean vent (rear-end) feathers with no smell.
- Straight toes and undamaged webs.
- Alert and active with no sign of lameness.

Ducks are less prone to infections than chickens. Most ailments are caused by poor husbandry, such as lack of water, overcrowding, or wet bedding. If you suspect an infestation of worms, contact your vet. Symptoms include lack of eggs, weight loss, and lethargy.

Saxony
This large, dual-purpose breed can lay reasonably well (about 150 eggs a year). A pretty, practical bird to keep, although the females can be noisy.

Indian Runner
A hardy duck, with an unusual upright stance. An excellent egg producer (about 300 eggs per year). Good natured, and average in terms of noise level.

Muscovy
Generally a gentle breed, and the quietest. The females make good mothers. Suitable for the table.

Khaki Campbell
A prolific egg layer: the best strains are capable of laying well over 300 eggs per year. A practical, reasonably quiet duck.

Rouen Clair
A large, docile, dual-purpose breed: a reasonable egg layer, and its meat is tasty. A relatively quiet bird.

Once you have decided on a suitable breed, contact your local organic poultry club to get more advice, and look through hobby farm magazines or go to waterfowl shows to find a suitable breeder. Always visit a breeder before buying any ducks.

Your ducks need to be taught where home is after you've bought them: to help them settle, keep new stock in a duck house with an outside run for a few days with plenty of clean straw, food, and fresh water. Then let the ducks out at the start of each day to roam freely until dusk, when they should be kept in again. Most domestic ducks don't fly, but you can stop a bird from flying by clipping the flight feather short on one wing.

Feeding your ducks

Ducks need fresh water and grass, grain, and grit to feed on. Grit is essential to help them digest their food, and if it's not available in your yard, supply it in a shallow box or a flower pot, in a dry place. Ducks will forage for their own food and add worms, insects, slugs, and snails to their normal grass and plant diet. If possible, move the duck house to a new area of grass every so often to reduce the risk of disease and the destruction of your lawn. You need only supplement the ducks' own foraging with a basic organic grain ration, provided first thing in the morning and at dusk in a feeder trough in the duck house. However, ducks that are laying or being fattened up for meat will need additional feeding with organic mixed corn and protein.

Duck eggs

Ducks will lay eggs from midwinter to midsummer, and a healthy duck will remain productive for around three years. To encourage good egg production, the darkest

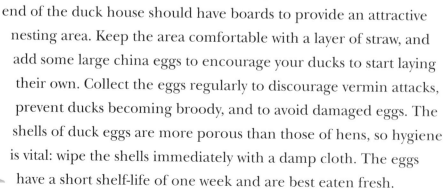

end of the duck house should have boards to provide an attractive nesting area. Keep the area comfortable with a layer of straw, and add some large china eggs to encourage your ducks to start laying their own. Collect the eggs regularly to discourage vermin attacks, prevent ducks becoming broody, and to avoid damaged eggs. The shells of duck eggs are more porous than those of hens, so hygiene is vital: wipe the shells immediately with a damp cloth. The eggs have a short shelf-life of one week and are best eaten fresh.

A duck keepers kit

1 Duck house
The house can be simple, but must be kept dry and clean (removable sides make this easy). Protect from dampness and rot with an organic wood preservative. Each bird needs 2 sq ft (60 sq cm) of roosting space.

2 Hose
Essential for keeping the floor of the duck house thoroughly clean.

3 Feeding hopper

4 Fresh water
Ducks need a constant supply of fresh drinking water.

5 Water to bathe in
A stream or clean pond is ideal, but a large, deep water trough, or a rigid plastic sandpit, with a ramp, is fine if it's cleaned regularly.

6 Feed
Organic mixed corn and protein can be bought in pellet form, or make your own mash from ground grains (oats, corn, and barley) and protein.

7 Fresh straw
Use straw or newspaper to keep the floor of the duck house dry.

USE UP A GLUT OF TOMATOES

Tomatoes are fully ripened and perfect for picking once they have turned a lovely rich red color. Home-grown tomatoes are full of delicious flavor and nutrition that's too good to waste, so if you have a large crop ripening at the same time, it's worth making soup or preserves that you can freeze or store for later in the year.

Tomato & fennel soup

(serves 4)

Ingredients

1 red onion, diced

1 tablespoon olive oil

4 cloves garlic, chopped

1 teaspoon fennel seed, ground

2 fennel bulbs, coarse outer leaves removed and sliced very thinly

2 lb (900 g) ripe tomatoes, quartered and deseeded

4 cups (1.2 liter) vegetable stock

1 teaspoon tomato purée

Salt and pepper

Method

■ Cook the onion in the olive oil in a large thick-based stainless steel pot until soft. Add the garlic and fennel seed. Cook for two minutes.

■ Add the sliced fennel bulbs, tomatoes, and the stock, bring to the boil, and simmer gently for 20 minutes.

■ Remove from the heat and stir in the tomato purée. Season with salt and pepper to taste and blend in a food processor. Leave to cool.

■ Decant into sealable containers and freeze.

Oven-dried tomatoes

The flavor of tomatoes is intensified by slowly roasting them in an oven. Cherry tomatoes are the easiest to use (yellow and red varieties work equally well), and cherry plum tomatoes are particularly good. It's worth preparing as many tomatoes as possible at a time, and use as much garlic and herbs as you like.

■ Preheat the oven to 200°F/145°C.

■ Lightly oil a baking tray with olive oil.

■ Cut a quantity of tomatoes in half and place them skin-side-down on a baking tray.

■ Finely slice some cloves of garlic and place them on top of the tomatoes. Sprinkle with finely chopped thyme or rosemary, a little sea salt, and a tiny amount of sugar. Put the tray in the oven.

■ Bake for about three hours. Check regularly that the tomatoes don't become dried out.

■ Store in a sealed container in the fridge. They will keep for about a week.

Tomato & chilli chutney

Ingredients

2 lb 4 oz (1 kg) ripe tomatoes

1 lb (500 g) onions, chopped

2 chilies, chopped

6 cloves garlic, chopped

1 lb (500 g) unrefined sugar

2 cups (500 ml) white wine vinegar

2 cups (500 ml) water

2 bay leaves

Salt and pepper

Method

■ Cut the tomatoes in half and scrape out the seeds and juice from the middle. Reserve the seeds and juice.

■ In a heavy-based saucepan, gently cook the onions, chili, and garlic in the oil until soft. Then add the tomato seeds and juice, along with the sugar, vinegar, water, and bay leaves.

■ Bring to the boil and simmer gently for about an hour or until reduced by half.

■ Roughly chop the tomato halves, season with salt and pepper, and add them to the pan.

■ Boil the chutney for a further 10 minutes, then remove the pan from the heat.

■ Sterilize some jars by washing them well and placing them in a moderate oven for five minutes. Then fill them with the chutney, secure the lids firmly, and store in a cool, dry place.

KEEP A GOAT OR TWO

Goats are relatively hardy animals, well-suited to many climates and ideal for a hobby farm. They can be kept for their good supplies of nutritious milk or reared for their low-fat meat. They are affectionate creatures but, given the slightest opportunity, they can create havoc in a yard.

Many people keep goats for their milk; goat's milk and cheese are becoming popular alternatives to traditional dairy foods made with cow's milk, which some people have an intolerance to. And in addition to milk and possibly meat, goat manure makes good organic fertilizer and the hair of some breeds can be turned into soft mohair, angora, or cashmere.

Goats are very sociable animals and love company, so you should plan to keep more than one unless you have other animals. Goats are related to sheep but, unlike sheep, they are not natural "lawn mowers" when it comes to grazing. Goats are choosy, and they can be obstinate, and may reject the finest meadow grass for a piece of paper or a weed that's just out of reach. They can also stand on their hind legs to reach leaves they particularly like to eat on bushes and small trees, and any plant can be a potential meal—including your flowers and vegetables. So you'll need to outwit your goats and keep them fenced in or tethered. They'll also need a dry shed to shelter from bad weather, plus fresh water and some additional feed.

Goat's milk

A goat needs to be pregnant to produce milk, and after the birth of kids it can give milk for almost a year. If the goat is not mated again, it can be milked for up to two years without interruption. Milk production increases with age: a mature nanny goat can give 7 pints (3.5 liters) of milk per day compared to a young nanny goat, which may give half this amount. Female goats come into season during their first fall; most have two kids, and give birth without much difficulty. You can then decide whether to keep or sell the kids.

Choose your goats

There are a range of breeds that a hobby farmer can consider. Choose your breed according to whether you want goats for their milk or meat. The productive life of a goat is about six years. Male goats reach sexual maturity at three months, when they can be used for meat.

Toggenburg
The smallest and most compact of the dairy breeds, originally from Switzerland. It can give good supplies of milk, and is extremely affectionate.

Anglo-Nubian
A short-coated variety with long drooping ears and a distinctive "Roman" nose. Produces high yields of rich milk, which is good for making cheese and yogurt.

If you want to keep goats for milk production, you must be prepared to milk them twice a day, every day, and give them regular attention. Neglect or irregularities in milking can quickly lead to health problems in milk goats. A milking goat should be fed and housed at night, and turned out to graze in between milking.

Keep your goats healthy

Goats need a secure area where they have some freedom and stimulation—preferably in the form of a scrambling area—plus a dry, draught-proof shelter, a balanced diet, and plenty of water. Goats are naturally healthy animals, and although they can be susceptible to some unpleasant conditions, good husbandry will help to prevent this.

Good levels of hygiene, clean food and water, and appropriate living conditions are the best protection against illness. As with any animal, keep an eye on a goat to identify any change in behavior or appearance. Call your vet if you spot any signs of injury, if the animal's eyes become dull, if it isn't eating or drinking normally, or if it stops producing milk.

Saanen
The largest of the Swiss goat breeds. Has a short, fine, white coat, pricked ears, and is usually hornless. Provides good supplies of milk.

Boer
A South African goat, the Boer goat is one of the few breeds specifically raised for meat production. It has characteristically large hanging ears.

Alpine
Mostly fawn-colored, although there are black and variegated varieties. Similar to the Saanen in form and milk production, but considered more robust.

It's essential to look after your goats' feet. The hooves of goats living in their original mountain habitats are constantly worn down by the rough rocks, but on a domestic hobby farm, they will need be trimmed on a regular basis and kept as dry as possible to prevent foot rot. Trim the hooves flat so that the goat can stand comfortably. If you are not able to trim them yourself with a sharp knife or foot trimmers, ask your vet to do it.

Like sheep, goats are susceptible to worms and coccidiosis. You can reduce the incidence of these infections by employing a "clean grazing" strategy, which requires areas used for grazing by goats in the spring to have been kept free from all animals for at least one year. Alternatively, you should ask your vet to worm your goats regularly. Remember that you shouldn't consume milk from wormed goats for at least seven days after worming. You should also regularly inspect your goats for lice, which will make them very uncomfortable and require treatment.

A goat keepers kit

1 Goat house
Each goat requires a minimum of 6 sq ft (2 sq m) of space inside a goat house or shed, which can also be used for milking. The shed should be tall enough for the goats to stand up on their hind legs with their necks outstretched. The shed should also be draught-proof.

2 Strong fencing
Goats will escape, given the opportunity, so they need to be tethered securely or confined behind strong, high fencing.

3 Mineral block
Fix a mineral lick to the wall of the goat house so that your goats get enough minerals in their diet.

4 Grazing area
Rough scrubland, hedges, and bushes all provide good grazing for goats. If possible, give them plenty of space to graze and roam around.

5 Fresh water
Goats need fresh supplies of water. Firmly securing a bucket of water down prevents a goat from kicking it over.

6 Secure areas
A bar above a stable-type open shed door will stop a goat from jumping out.

7 Feed
As well as grass, goats need rations of grain and hay, which must be available at all times. Secure the hay racks with bars to stop goats from pulling out too much hay at once. Milking goats need extra feed of concentrates, such as flaked corn, rolled oats, or crushed beans.

Basic equipment

Unlike sheep and cattle, which can stay out in all weathers, goats need a dry shed where they can shelter from the wet and cold. A wooden or concrete floor is best, covered with comfortable bedding. Ideally, the house should have a concrete yard attached so that the goats have some freedom outside in bad weather.

Good strong fences are essential; normal barbed wire or netting fences are not adequate. To restrain goats, use either chain link fences (at least 4 ft/1.2 m high) with barbed wire, or three to four strands of electric fence (at least 3 ft 6 in/1 m high).

If you tether a goat, keep a constant eye on her: provide water, protecte her from other animals such as dogs, and move her out of the sun or rain.

Feeding

Goats will forage for about half of their diet and eat shrubs, gorse, and brambles. They will also eat any vegetable scraps you can provide. While they are being milked, they also need about 2–4 lb (1–2 kg) of a concentrate ration, and 2–4 lb (1–2 kg) of hay and roots per day during the winter months. Kid goats need about 2 pints (1.2 liter) of milk for the first two to three months, before being weaned onto a diet of hay and concentrate. The feed should be placed in troughs at goat head-height in the goat house so that the goats can reach it, but not foul it. A ready supply of clean drinking water is also essential.

MAKE A SIMPLE GOAT'S CHEESE

The fresh, tangy flavor of goat's cheese is a wonderful addition to a cheese board. It's much easier to make soft cheese than it is to make hard cheese, and different herbs can be added to enhance the flavor.

The principle of making milk into cheese is simple: the milk is soured with a bacterial culture, then rennet (an enzyme from the stomach of cows) is added, which causes curds to form—the basic ingredient of cheese. The cheese is separated from the whey, then salted and dried.

- Warm 1 gallon (4.5 liters) of fresh goat's milk in a large pan to 90°F (32°C).
- Stir in the starter, a bacterial culture that creates acidity. Either buy the starter

or make it: the basic method consists of leaving some unpasteurized milk (approx ½ cup/125 ml) to turn sour.

■ Leave to stand for 45 minutes, then add rennet (according to the instructions on the packet). The curds may take 12 hours to coagulate fully. When the curds split easily if you push your finger through them, they are ready.

■ Strain the curds through cheesecloth (which should be scalded to prevent the cheese from going bad) to drain off the whey. Tie the corners of the cloth together and hang the curds to drain overnight.

■ Add a little salt to taste. Use the fresh curds as cheese, or put the curds into molds lined with cheesecloth and leave weights on top. More whey will drain out, so the cheeses will become firmer.

■ If you wish, roll the shaped cheeses in finely chopped fresh herbs of your choice, or nuts, and store in the fridge.

PLANT A VINE

With its thick woody stem and large leaves that turn burnished shades in the fall, a grapevine (*Vitis vinifera*) is a wonderful, vigorous climber to grow in a garden. It will scramble over pergolas to create shady areas, or decorate walls or fences.

If you plant a vine in a sunny corner in well-drained soil and leave it to its own devices, it will produce some bunches of edible grapes, although eventually the leaves will take over and there'll be less fruit. If you're prepared to take a bit of time choosing the right variety and train it and prune it every year, then you should be rewarded with the first of countless bunches of fully flavored grapes for the table, for juice, or for winemaking just three years after planting. A well-tended vine can produce top-quality grapes for 40 years or more.

Growing grapes organically will guarantee that they have not been sprayed with chemicals, as most supermarket ones are, and picking them when fully ripe will give you the sweetest of fruits. Vines are not fussy plants, and once they establish their root systems, they get the moisture and nutrients they need from deep in the soil. They won't survive in waterlogged soil, however, or produce good fruit in nitrogen-rich soil. While the bunches of fruit hang on the stems, they won't ripen fully unless the temperature is at least 50°F (10°C) .

Most vines prefer:

■ **Well-drained soil** free from perennial weeds, with a pH (this measures its acidity) of 6.3–6.8. Ideally, the soil should be prepared before planting by digging in garden compost, with added grit on heavy soils. Some varieties will not grow well in alkaline soils.

■ **A sunny site** less than 650 ft (200 m) above sea level: in temperate climates, plant against a wall or fence that faces south, southeast, or southwest, with the planting hole at least 6 in (15 cm) from the base. Vines need dry, warm weather at flowering time to set fruit.

■ **Regular watering** when newly planted, to encourage the roots to grow down and out into the soil.

Varieties to grow outdoors

Grapes need plenty of warmth to ripen fully outdoors. In cooler areas, it's best to grow early ripening dessert varieties—very late ripening ones, such as Black Hamburg, need the extra warmth and protection of a greenhouse. Grapes are susceptible to various fungal diseases so it is worth choosing ones that have the greatest resistance to disease.

Dessert grapes/white wines

1. Siegerrebe
2. Himrod
3. Madeleine Angevine
4. Seibel

Dessert grapes/red wines

5. Regent
6. Leon Millot
7. Triomphe d'Alsace
8. Boskoop Glory

Buying & planting a vine

Vines for sale in specialist nurseries are usually grafted onto phylloxera-resistant rootstock (phylloxera is a pest that attacks the roots of vines. In the nineteenth century, it almost wiped out all the vines in Europe). It's a good idea to choose your plants from a specialist grower and get advice on the best varieties and how to train and prune them. Dessert grapes are larger than wine grapes and rarely make good wine. Some wine grapes, however, are sweet enough to eat.

Vines climb by tendrils and need support. They can be grown free-standing on wires supported by sturdy posts and trained horizontally and vertically against the wires. Or they can be grown up posts and trained into heart or goblet shapes, over a wheel or up and over a pergola. A vine against a wall should be trained up a pole and onto heavy galvanized wires with a 1½ in (4 cm) gap behind them.

How vines are trained depends on the grape variety and on factors such as walls or doors in a wall. Whatever the method, a vine should be cut back hard on planting, and again at the end of the first season. The purpose of pruning, which should be done every winter (and with some lighter pruning and thinning in summer), encourages the plant to produce regular crops of good-sized grapes. For dessert grapes, special scissors with long thin blades are useful for snipping off some of the smaller bunches to allow larger bunches more space and light.

Picking ripe grapes

Grapes start to ripen once they change from green. It's best to leave them on the vine until the sugar content increases fully—this can take anything from a few weeks to a couple of months, depending on the variety. The best way to test their ripeness is to taste them. Traditionally grapes are cut with enough stalk to make a "T" shape so that they can be carried without being touched. Handling the grapes damages the "bloom"—the waxy coating on the skins—which helps to protect the fruits and deflects rain water while they grow.

HELP WILDLIFE SURVIVE IN THE WINTER

Many of the insects and other small creatures that live in yards hibernate through the cold winter months, so they need safe, weatherproof places to hide in. They also need plenty of food in the fall in order to fatten up before becoming inactive. Other wildlife, such as birds and larger mammals, that keep going through winter need regular supplies of food and drinking water. You can help all the wildlife in your yard to survive for another season by being aware of what they need and making sure that you provide it.

Plan ahead

■ **Leave some part of the yard undisturbed** where insects and other small creatures can take shelter. This can be an area of tall grass, a pile of leaves or decaying plants, or plant stems left standing through the winter months.

■ **Grow berrying and fruiting plants** in your yard, including some species such as hawthorn, blackthorn, rowan, crab apple, elder, ivy, pyracantha, cotoneaster, rugosa rose, and bramble. These plants will provide a supply of food for birds and small mammals.

■ **Leave seed heads** of plants such as teasel, sunflowers, and fennel standing so that seed eaters such as finches can help themselves. Seed heads can also provide winter quarters for some bugs.

■ **Make a pile of logs** or sticks in a quiet spot to provide a wintering site for a community of animals from pill bugs, spiders, and hoverflies to toads, frogs, and salamanders. If you bury the logs at the bottom of the pile in the soil, many different beetle species may even take up residence in the decaying wood.

Extra help for birds

Putting out extra food on bird tables and in feeders during the winter months can be a lifesaver for many birds, especially in city gardens and when there is snow on the ground. The more feeders the better, and a variety of foods will attract different species.

Black sunflower seeds are one of the best all-around foods—use shelled sunflower seeds if you don't want a scattering of husks under the feeder. Goldfinches will flock to eat nyjer seeds, while house sparrows, chickadees, and greenfinches enjoy peanuts. Put the whole nuts in wire mesh feeders so that they can't be fed to young birds. Avoid salty food and stale bread, which can be harmful. Some birds, such as the cardinal, junco, and sparrow, prefer to find their food on the ground. To feed these birds, make or buy a low table and cover it with a protective cage. Bird tables should be cleaned with a mild detergent from time to time to prevent infections from spreading. Fresh water for drinking and bathing is vital, too. In freezing weather, keep a birdbath from icing over completely by floating a ball on the surface, or defrost it using hot water.

Nesting sites

From early spring onward, birds need nesting sites. The trunks of mature trees, thick leafy climbers, hedges, and holes in walls all provide natural sites. You can also offer extra nests by putting up boxes, either open-fronted for birds such as robins and wrens, or hole-fronted for bluebirds, starlings, house sparrows, nuthatches, and owls. It is easy and cheap to make your own nestin box using pieces of weatherproofed wood and galvanized screws and nails, or you can buy one of the huge range of ready-made ones. Put up nest boxes in the fall, and position them out of strong sunlight and driving rain, so that the birds have plenty of time to find them.

Food & shelter for squirrels

Squirrels do not hibernate during the winter months. If there is heavy snow cover, or very cold snaps, they will stay in their dens for extended periods of time. However, to make it through the winter, squirrels must still venture out to look for food. You can help squirrels out by making sure that birdfeeders are well and regularly stocked with sunflower seeds, for example, throughout the winter.

Insect homes

To encourage lots of beneficial insects such as ladybugs, lacewings, and bees to stay on in your gardens or yard, you can easily make hibernation homes for them. Cut up short lengths of bamboo poles or hollow plant stems, cram them into an open-fronted box or tube, and hang the tube in a sheltered spot. There are also ready-made versions of these shelters available to buy. For solitary bees and wasps, drill holes of different sizes in pieces of wood. Then position your bee and wasp homes in areas where the insects' activities will not disturb you while you are in the garden.

Did you know

● In Britain, 700 species of beetle live off decaying wood. More than half of these species are rare or threatened.

● Grass snakes sometimes use compost heaps as nesting sites. The warmth of the rotting vegetation provides ideal conditions for incubating their eggs.

● In response to the colder air temperatures of winter, a hedgehog's body temperature drops from around 35°C to 10°C or less while it is hibernating.

PLANT & SOW BY THE MOON

For organic gardeners, the key to growing healthy, strong plants is fertile soil that has good structure and supplies of nutrients. Some gardeners believe that the moon plays a vital role in plant growth and development, too. They hold that the moon's gravitational pull, to which scientists attribute the rise and fall of the Earth's oceans, also affects the Earth's water table, causing increased amounts of moisture to move up into the topsoil. The period from a new moon to a full moon (the waxing moon), when increased moisture is available to seeds and plants, is the best time to sow and plant. The period from a full moon to the next new moon (the waning moon), when the moisture content is at its lowest and there's less sap rising in trees and shrubs, is the time to prune.

To benefit from these lunar influences of the moon, people who practice gardening by the moon draw up an annual calendar and tend their plants accordingly. Biodynamic gardeners and farmers, who follow the teachings of Austrian philosopher Rudolph Steiner, also use lunar calendars, but theirs are more complex, as they believe that plants are affected by wider planetary rhythms, and that crops are linked to one of the four traditional elements—earth, water, air, and fire—depending on whether they are root, leaf, flower, or seed crops. Each crop must be planted when the moon is in the sign of the zodiac associated with that element.

Biodynamic gardening methods involve keeping the soil full of vitality by adding compost and manure and special therapeutic preparations made from plant, mineral, and animal material. Crops grown this way, it is claimed, are more vigorous and taste better.

CREATE A POND FOR WILDLIFE

The pressure on land for agriculture, housing, and commercial development has meant that many ponds and wetlands that native wildlife depend on are becoming polluted or have been drained. Garden ponds are important havens for these creatures, so a pond designed and made with wildlife in mind, and planted with the right plants, will soon be colonized by a host of creatures—from tiny water organisms and plankton to visiting birds and mammals.

Snails and small crustaceans will arrive on birds' feet or attached to plants; diving beetles, water fleas, water boatmen, and pond skaters may soon be spotted scurrying through the water; insects such as dragonflies and damselflies will fly in and start to breed; and birds will fly down to drink and bathe. Later, frogs, toads, and newts may take up residence, and mammals such as foxes and raccoons could become regular visitors.

Any container of fresh water will attract some wildlife, but a specially designed pond is one of the best ways of providing for a wide variety of creatures. Site the pond in a spot where plants have enough sunlight to grow.

Wildlife ponds can be different shapes, sizes, and depths, but they all need:
- Clean water with low levels of nutrients.
- Shallow edges that shelve, to allow different plants to flourish and creatures to climb or crawl out of the pond easily.
- An area of pond that is 24 in (60 cm) deep so that creatures can survive hot summers and freezing winters.
- Plant cover that includes some native species to create shade and shelter—about two-thirds plants to one-third open water is ideal.

How to make a wildlife pond

● Decide on the size and shape of the pond and mark it out with a hose or some sand. Site it away from large trees, as their roots may disturb or pierce the pond base, and fallen leaves lying on the water can deplete it of oxygen as they decay. Dig the hole with gently sloping shelves around the sides.

● Remove any sharp stones, roots, or debris. Line the base with a layer of sand or matting, then lay down the liner, leaving extra around the sides so that the edges can be buried under turf or other edging such as stone slabs or pebbles. Use a good-quality strong rubber or plastic liner that won't tear (buy the liner from a pond supplier). Alternatively, line the base with puddled clay.

● Fill the hole with water. The weight of the water will mold the liner to the shape of the pond. Hide the edges of the liner under the grass or other edging. If using tap water, allow it to stand for 48 hours before planting or introducing wildlife. For a good balance of water wildlife, don't stock the pond with fish. Even small sticklebacks are voracious and will devor spawn and adult insects.

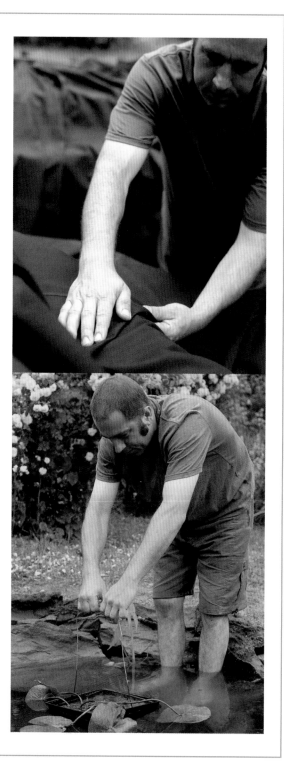

Planting in a pond

Pond life is adapted to native plants, so include a variety of these, as well as any exotics you might like. (Some non-native plants can be difficult to eradicate once they get established, and choke up ponds and rivers, so be careful what you plant.) Introduce rooted plants in mesh baskets and cover the soil or compost in the basket with gravel to prevent it washing away.

Free-floating submerged plants help to oxygenate the water and give hiding places to deeper water creatures. Examples are curly pondweed *(Potamogeton crispus)*, Eurasian water milfoil *(Myriophyllum spicatum)*, and common hornwort *(Ceratophyllum demersum)*.

Floating plants rest their leaves on the surface of the water and help to provide shade and cover. Examples are yellow yellow pond lily *(Nuphar lutea)*, frogbit *(Hydrocharis morsus-ranae)*, ribbon-leaved pondweed *(Potamogeton natans)*, and water soldier *(Stratiotes aloides)*.

Shallow water plants, many of which have attractive flowers, provide stems for emerging nymphs to climb up and roots where invertebrates can shelter. Examples are buckbean *(Menyanthes trifoliata)*, true forget-me-not *(Myosotis scorpioides)*, and pale yellow iris *(Iris pseudacorus)*.

Pond-edge flowering plants provide nectar for butterflies, bees, and other insects. Examples are marsh marigold *(Caltha palustris)*, ragged robin *(Lychnis flos-cuculi)*, and meadowsweet *(Filipendula ulmaria)*.

Tips on pond care

- Skim off duckweed (*Lemna* species) when it gets too dense.

- Rake off or scoop out leaves from the surface of the water.

- In hot weather, top up the pond, ideally with rain water.

- In winter, pull and lift out any plants that are taking over and cut back any dead plants.

- In freezing weather float a ball on the pond to prevent all the water icing over. Take out the ball to create an air hole for pond creatures.

- After removing blanket weed, leave it at the side of the pond for 24 hours to allow any small creatures in it to return to the water. Clear only a quarter of the weed at a time to allow wildlife to get used to changes in light and oxygen.

- Don't expect crystal-clear water. Green water means that it is full of algae, but the water turns a natural brownish color once small water creatures start to feed on it. You can speed up this process by introducing some water fleas (Daphnia species) from an established pond. If this doesn't work, throw in a net of barley straw. For the correct amount, check with a specialist aquatic center.

RAISE A COUPLE OF YOUNG PIGS

Pigs are intelligent and sensitive creatures, but they are also hardy, versatile animals that flourish well in a hobby farm, eating up household food scraps, foraging for themselves, and providing an efficient source of meat and fertilizer.

Originally descended from woodland foraging creatures, today's domestic pigs are one of the most productive of all livestock animals for converting feed to meat, as well as producing valuable manure for the hobby farmer. They can rotavate ground effectively or, if kept in orchards, they will control the weeds, fertilize the soil, and eat up the windfalls.

In addition, pigs are friendly and sociable animals, and it's easy for you and your family to form bonds with them. Unfortunately, this may make parting with them difficult when the time comes to send them to the slaughterhouse. On the positive side, breeding your own pigs for meat provides a good source of delicious pork, bacon, and sausages, and possibly some extra income. Pigs are ready to be slaughtered at 26 weeks old, but they need to be kept and fed for about ten months if they are to be used for bacon.

Where to start

It is a good idea to begin by visiting local agricultural shows and talking to pig farmers and other hobby farmers before you start looking for a reputable breeder. In this way, you can build up your knowledge before you buy any livestock. Hobby farm magazines are also a good source of information on potential

Signs of good health in a pig

Don't go for looks unless you are interested in buying pedigree pigs. Instead, buy pigs with good, easy-going temperaments. Signs of good health include:

● A moist snout.

● Bright eyes—if the pig's ears cover its eyes, look underneath the ears to check the eyes.

● A shiny coat, with the hairs lying close to the body (a dull coat can be a sign of illness).

● A curly tail; a straight tail may indicate illness.

A lack of appetite, loss of energy, lameness, scouring, or diarrhea could indicate an infection or disease.

stock to buy. Before you do consider buying, check that you can provide your pigs with the right shelter, enough space, and some soil to dig around in.

Always keep at least two pigs, as they love company. Perhaps the best, and cheapest, way to start is to buy young pigs, or "weaners," which are weaned from their mothers at around six to eight weeks old. Pigs at this age can be trained and handled more easily, and are easier to introduce to the food you'll feed them on. Older pigs are more fussy. Another option is to purchase a sow "in pig," meaning that she will soon give birth to a litter of piglets. Keeping a sow is essential if you intend to breed your own pigs as a source of meat and income.

Choose your pigs

The type of pig you buy depends on how you will want to use or sell the meat. Some pigs are ideal for dual-purpose use: in other words, they can be kept for both pork and bacon. The older and less developed the breed, the hardier it will be; such breeds are easy for a hobby farmer to keep. These are some of the most suitable breeds.

Large White
A popular modern breed, now used widely because of its productivity. Can get sunburned outside in warm climates.

Saddleback
A rare and distinctive-looking breed. Good maternal instincts. Dual-purpose (there is a slight discoloration of the meat).

Large Black
A rare, hardy breed that copes in cold temperatures. A good pasture feeder and breeder. Bred primarily for bacon.

Tamworth
A rare, very old breed with a golden-red coat. Ideal for outdoor rearing, it is hardy and a good rotavator. Dual-purpose.

Middle White
A rare, hardy breed that is alert and curious, but also docile. A consistently good breeder and bred for its pork.

Gloucestershire Old Spot
A rare breed at home in a cold climate. It breeds and forages well and has a good temperament. Dual-purpose.

Hampshire
A hardy American breed similar to the Saddleback. A good breeder and forager. Easy to handle, despite its large size.

Berkshire
A rare breed with a black coat, white feet, a white face, and white tail tip. Copes well in cold temperatures. Bred for pork.

Duroc
A hardy American breed originally bred for lard. A good breeder with a docile temperament. Bred for bacon.

Caring for your pigs

Pigs aren't demanding animals, but they do need regular attention and more space than you might assume. They need to be fed twice a day, must have warm, dry shelter and require sufficient dirt and water to dig around and bathe in.

The best environment

For really healthy and happy pigs, you should allow them enough space to roam around and dig in open ground. An area of around 360 sq yds (300 sq m) is preferable for two pigs. The ground should be dry and not marshy, with good drainage. Avoid stony ground, as pigs have a tendency to hurt their feet on stones and rocks. Pigs don't need to feed on the best grass, and will eradicate weeds and help plow the soil. Ideally, if you can, allow them to forage in an orchard or in woodland, which will provide them with food and plenty of interest.

Basic requirements

Pigs need soil and grass for the vitamins and minerals they contain, and they like to dig and forage for worms. They also need a pool of water, or water hole, to bathe in. A coating of mud helps to protect the pigs' skin from sunburn and keep them cool in the sun. Fill up their baths regularly with clean water in hot weather, or even hose them down on particularly hot days.

Pigs are intelligent animals and can get bored in a small space, so give them as large an area to live in as possible, secured with two lines of electric fencing (4 in/10 cm and 8 in/20 cm above the ground) or pig netting fixed to strong posts. Move your pigs to new ground when they have exhausted supplies of grass and grubs to reduce the chances of worms or other ailments.

Pigs also need warm, dry areas to shelter from harsh weather, to sleep in, and to bear piglets. These need only be simple structures that can be easily moved, and you can buy them or make them yourself. Provide the pigs with a comfortable bed of clean straw regularly.

Feeding

As well as eating grass and clover, and worms and nutrients in the soil, pigs need a supplement of soy bean and corn-based feed and water to drink. You can also feed them wheat, barley, and fruit and vegetable scraps, although some vegetables, such as potatoes, should be cooked. Don't give them any feed containing animal meat. If you have any spare or waste 2 percent or skim milk, however, pigs will love this added to their cereal. Feed your pigs twice a day at the same time; if you don't, they will notice and become irritable.

Settling your pigs into their new home

When you bring your pigs home, keep them in a small pen with a shelter, or a sty, for a few days. Give them lots of fresh water and feed them twice a day until they are used to the routine. Then let them out to graze.

A pig keeper's kit

1 **Shelter or arc**
A basic hut made from simple materials, such as iron or wood, will enable a pig to shelter from sun and rain and house any piglets she may have.

2 **Hose**
Use a hose to top up the pigs' water holes or wallowing area.

3 **Fresh water**
All pigs need a constant supply of clean, fresh water to drink, but sows in milk need even more. Fix the water trough securely to the ground and make sure that the piglets can reach over the rim to drink the water.

4 **Household scraps**
Pigs will happily eat household scraps (they should never be given meat).

5 **Straw**
Provide plenty of straw for the pig sty or shelter at least once a month.

6 **Feed**
One of the best feed for pigs is soaked barley meal and "middlings" or "sharps"—a fine wheat bran.

4 DIRECTORY

DIRECTORY

Babies & Children

Babywear and children's clothes
Gaiam www.gaiam.com
Naturally Suite www.naturallysuite.com

Diapers
www.motherease.com Tel 1.800.416.1475

Energy
Energy-saving gadgets
Natural Collection Gadgets for the home that save energy. **www.naturalcollection.com**

Information on renewable systems, solar systems, and renewable energy resources available throughout the US
US Department of Energy Energy Efficiency and Renewable Energy
General information on green energy.
www.eere.energy.gov

Alternative Energy Systems Co.
1469 Rolling Hills Road, Conroe, TX, 77303
Tel 936.264.4873

Database of State Incentives for Renewable Energy (DSIRE)
DSIRE is a comprehensive source of information on state, local, utility, and federal incentives that promote renewable energy and energy efficiency across the United States.
http://www.dsireusa.org

Alternate Energy Technologies
OEM Thermafin copper absorber plates and flat plate solar thermal collectors. Tel 1.800.874.2190

Wind energy
Information on wind and hydro power programs and systems. **www.eere.energy.gov/windandhydro/**

American Wind Energy Trade Association
www.awea.org/

Calculate your energy costs
Links to home energy and appliance use calculators
www.eere.energy.gov/consumer/calculators/homes.cfm

Green energy suppliers
Links to utility companies providing green electricity alternatives and initiatives.
www.ecobusinesslinks.com/green_electricity_providers_sustainable_power_companies.htm

Energy Outfitters Ltd
Solar, wind, hydroelectric, and other "green" systems
453 NE East Street, Grants Pass, OR 97562
www.energyoutfitters.com

Green-e Certification
Green-e is the most respected independent renewable energy certification and verification program in the United States. The Green-e logo helps consumers quickly identify environmentally sound energy options and is used by businesses to

communicate the purchase and/or generation of certified renewable energy. **www.green-e.org**

Energy-saving light bulbs and other eco-friendly products
www.ecomall.com

Small wind turbines
www.bergey.com
www.energy.sourceguides.com

Solar yard/garden lights
www.solarbuzz.com

Environmental Issues
Global Cool is a campaign to slash carbon dioxide emissions by 1 billion tons.
www.globalcool.com

Food & Drink

TransFairUSA
Nonprofit organization, one of 20 members of Fairtrade Labeling Organizations International (FLO), and the only third-party certifier of Fair Trade products in the US.
1611 Telegraph Ave. Suite 900, Oakland, CA 94612
info@transfairusa.org Tel 510.663.5260

Farmers' markets
A comprehensive list of farmers' markets.
www.ams.usda.gov/farmersmarkets/

Fruit & vegetable box schemes
www.allorganiclinks.com

Online fish suppliers
Aqua Find **www.aquafind.com**
Northern Aquaculture
www.northernaquaculture.com

Online fresh meat suppliers
Organic Bison **www.FiveHerds.com**
Laura's Lean Beef **www.laurasleanbeef.com**

Organic drinks
www.just-drinks.com
www.naturalfoodnet.com

Organic wines
www.fourchimneysorganicwines.com
www.valleywineandspirits.com

Yard & Garden

Gardens Alive
A wide range of organic gardening and farming supplies. **www.gardensalive.com**

National Pesticide-free Lawns Coalition
This organization supports pesticide-free lawn and landscaping projects. **www.beyondpesticides.org**

Nematode suppliers
www.bugladyconsulting.com
www.extremelygreen.com

Composting
Worm composters recycle 70% of household waste.
www. homeharvest.com
www.composters.com

Fungi

www.fungusamongus.com

www.mycosupply.com

www.fungi.com

Herbs

www.KitchenGardeners.org

Fruit trees and orchard supplies

Adams County Nursery www.acnursery.com

Bountiful Gardens

Gardening equipment, and organic vegetable and herb seeds. **www.bountifulgardens.org**

The Cook's Garden

Specializes in gourmet and heirloom vegetables and flowers. **www.cooksgarden.com**

Ed Hume Seeds, Inc.

Seeds for short seasons and cool climates. **www.humeseeds.com**

Edible Landscaping

Specializes in a wide range of fruits. **www.eat-it.com**

Irish Eyes Garden City Seeds

Specializes in seeds for potatoes, onions, and garlic. **www.irish-eyes.com**

Lehman's

Non-electric appliances, tools, grain mills, and more. **www.lehmans.com**

Native Seeds/SEARCH

Southwestern native and heirloom vegetable and herb seeds. **www.nativeseeds.com**

Natural Gardening Company

A wide range of organic gardening supplies. **www.naturalgardening.com**

Nichols Garden Nursery

Untreated herb and vegetable seeds. **www.nicholsgardennursery.com**

Park Seed Company

Huge selection of vegetable, herb, and flower seeds. **www.parkseed.com**

Pintree Garden Seeds

Inexpensive, small seed packets and many other gardening-related products. **www.superseeds.com**

Raintree Nursery

Specializes in fruits, nuts, and edible plants. **www.raintreenursery.com**

Seed Savers Exchange

Specializes in heirloom vegetables, and is home of the Flower and Herb Exchange. **www.seedsavers.org**

Seeds Trust High Altitude Gardens

Specializes in seeds for high altitudes and cold climates. **www.seedstrust.org**

Southern Exposure Seed Exchange

Open-pollinated and heirloom vegetable, flower, and herb seeds. **www.southernexposure.com**

Home

Soy wax and organic candles

www.mrsmyers.com

www.pristineplanet.com

Cleaning products

Seventh Generation

Leading eco-friendly cleaning product company; products are widely available in grocery stores, and via the website. **www.seventhgeneration.com**

Other biodegradable cleaning products

www.worxbest.com

www.treecycle.com

www.ecover.com/us

Eco-friendly clothing

www.gaiam.com

www.pangaya.com

www.ecomall.com

www.pristineplanet.com

Organic hemp clothing. **www.hemptraders.com**

Eco-friendly shoes

www.rawganique.com

www.softstarshoes.com

www.skinet.com

Housing materials

Living roofs incorporate a shallow soil base covered in sedum and other plants to attract wildlife.

www.greenroofs.com

www.earthpledge.org/s

www.greenroofplants.com

Presents

www.ecomall.com

www.pristineplanet.com

Reclaimed, recycled, and environmentally friendly furniture and home accessories

www.ecoterric.com

www.naturalcollection.com

www.celticvikingfurniture.com

www.HipandZen.com

www.greensage.com

www.abundantearth.com

Feminine hygiene products

www.omplace.com

www.manymoons.biz

Toiletries

www.naturalcollection.com

Hemp and beeswax toiletries:

www.herbnet.com

www.natureswildchild.com

www.burtsbees.com

Livestock

Compassion in World Farming

This UK-based organization aims to stop cruel and inhumane practices in farming around the world. **www.ciwf.org**

Bees

Beekeeping laws and regulations vary widely from state to state, and city to city. For information on your state's laws and other matters related to beekeeping from the following organizations:

American Beekeeping Federation
www.abfnet.org
American Honey Producers Organization
www.americanhoneyproducers.org
Bee Culture The magazine of American beekeeping
www.beeculture.com

Chickens

Regulations: There are no regulations governing flocks under 250 birds, and you don't need planning permission for small, movable chicken housing, but contact your local Environmental Health Officer to check local bylaws. Also check for news on avian influenza and possible regulations. You can only sell eggs to retailers if you're a registered producer.

Backyard Poultry
Small flock poultry breeding and keeping information.
www.backyardpoultrymag.com

American Poultry Association
www.ampltya.com

The American Pastured Poultry Producers Association
Assists all pasture raised poultry in the US.
www.apppa.org

Mother Earth News: Chicken and Egg Page
Wonderful resource for information on all of the subjects in this book, with pages on keeping free-range chickens. www.motherearthnews.com

The City Chicken
Helps all those who want to raise poultry in their backyards. www.thecitychicken.com

Cows

Regulations and bylaws: Check all federal or local regulations governing the keeping of cattle.

Books on raising cattle
Book titles for everything related to raising cattle.
www.cattlebooks.com

Backwoods Home Magazine
Online magazine for those living a self-reliant lifestyle, including raising cattle in small spaces.
www.backwoodshome.com

American Association of Bovine Practitioners
This international association of veterinarians helps with issues critical to cattle industries and issues.
www.aabp.org

The American Veterinary Medical Association
www.avma.org

Ducks

Regulations and bylaws: Check federal or local regulations governing the keeping of ducks, and news on avian influenza and possible regulations.

Feather Site
www.feathersite.com

The New Agrarian
Essays related to hobby farms and has a helpful page

on keeping ducks in suburban or rural areas.
www.newagrarian.com

Soil Science Society of America
This organization aims to advance the discipline and practice of soil science **www.soils.org**

American Pheasant and Waterfowl Society
www.upatsix.com

The University of Minnesota Extension Service
www.extension.umn.edu

Geese
For information related to raising geese, ducks, and swans **www.gamebird.com**

The University of Minnesota Extension Service
www.extension.umn.edu

Goats
Regulations: Goats are covered by animal welfare regulations. Contact the US Department of Agriculture Animal Welfare Regulations for more details. **www.nal.usda.gov**

Farm Info
A small farm resource, including comprehensive information on goats. **www.farminfo.org**

The American Goat Society
www.americangoatsociety.com

The American Dairy Goat Society
www.adga.org

Pigs
Regulations: Pigs are also covered by animal welfare regulations. Contact the US Department of Agriculture Animal Welfare Regulations for more details. **www.nal.usda.gov**

The Pig Site
Links to pig-related websites and vital pig information **www.thepigsite.com**

North American Potbellied Pig Association
www.petpigs.com

American Veterinary Medical Association
www.avma.org

Recycling
For more information on recycling your waste.
National Recycling Coalition www.nrc-recycle.org

Knowaste
Diaper recycling **www.knowaste.com**

Earth 911
Links to local recycling resources and centers, and information on water pollution and conservation.
www.earth911.org

Transportation
Hybrid cars
Hybrid models produce 75% less pollution than a standard ultra-low emission car. For general information. **www.hybridcars.com**

Electric cars

Check out these information-packed websites:

www.eaaev.org

www.electricdrive.org

Global Electric Motorcars (GEM)

www.gemcar.com

Carpooling

Matches you to local carpools in your area.

www.carpoolworld.com

Association for Commuter Transportation

www.actweb.org

Bicycle routes and US-based adventure vacations

GORP: Adventure Travel and Outdoor Recreation

Links to various regional biking routes and paths.

www.gorp.away.com/gorp/activity/biking.htm

Bicycling routes, trails, and maps

www.pedaling.com

Adventure Cycling Association

www.adv-cycling.org

Carbon footprint

To calculate the carbon emissions you create go to

www.myfootprint.org

www.carbonfootprint.com

www.conservation.org

www.safeclimate.net

Water

Toilet watersaver devices such as toilet dams, which save 2-3 gallons per flush, are available at:

www.care2.greenhome.com

General information on water conservation:

www.epa.gov

www.americanrivers.org

www.uswaternews.com

Water Environment Federation

This organization is devoted to preserving and enhancing the global water environment.

www.wef.org

Wildlife

The following websites offer information on how to help protect America's wildlife:

World Wildlife Fund www.worldwildlife.org

Animal Charities of America

Nonprofit organization that pre-screens animal related charities.

www.AnimalCharitiesofAmerica.org

National Wildlife Federation

The mission of the NWF is to inspire Americans to protect wildlife for our children's future.

www.nwf.org

Other books on organic living

The Living Soil
Lady Eve Balfour; Faber and Faber, 1933
One of the definitive books on the health-giving powers of the organic management of soil and garden. Lady Balfour was effectively one of the founders of the reborn "organic" movement.

Short Circuit
Richard Douthwaite; Green Books 1996
A useful and comprehensive collection of alternative economic systems which bring back control to a more local level. There is also a powerful statement explaining the importance of adopting more of such systems.

Blueprint for A Green Planet
John Seymour and Herbert Girardet, Dorling Kindersley, 1987
Comprehensive and common sense review of actions that could be taken in all the routing activities of daily life to save the future of the planet. Full of neat diagrams and plenty of frightening facts about the consequences of our present Western approach to ordinary living.

The Gaia Atlas of Planetary Management
Norman Myers; Pan Books, 1985
This is an ideal book to give younger people a good idea

Organic Gardening
Maria Rodale; Rodale Press, Emmaus, PA 18098, 1999
An inspirational book celebrating the beauty of organic growing and discussin many of its leading ideas.

The Organic Garden Book
Geoff Hamilton, Dorling Kindersley, 1987
For growing better tasting fruit and vegetables untainted by chemicals—written by a much missed man.

Rodale's Illustrated Encyclopedia of Organic Gardening
Edited by Anna Kruger, Dorling Kindersley, 2005
Comprehensive advice on all aspects of organic gardening, including composting, soil care, and growing your own fruit and vegetables.

Organic Baby and Toddler Cookbook
Lizzie Vann and Daphne Razazan, Dorling Kindersley, 2001
Healthy meals made from fresh, additive-free natural ingredients for your baby and child.

INDEX

Page numbers in italics indicate a boxed entry. Entries in italics indicate a recipe or a Latin plant name. Latin names are not given for vegetables, fruit, and herbs.

ACKNOWLEDGMENTS

The publisher would like to thank the following for their kind permission to reproduce their photographs:
(a-above; b-below/bottom; c-centre; f-far; l-left; r-right; t-top)
9 Anthony Blake Photo Library: Ming Tang Evans. **21 GAP Photos Ltd:** John Glover (tr); Maddie Thornhill (tl) (cb). **Garden World Images:** T. McGlinchey (br). **62 Alamy Images:** Pat Tuson (br). **FLPA:** Nigel Cattlin (cl) (cr); Foto Natura Stock (c); Tony Wharton (bc). **63 FLPA:** Nigel Cattlin (cr) (cl). Garden Picture Library: David Cavagnaro (bl). Garden World Images: H. Harrison (bc). **73 Garden Picture Library:** Friedrich Strauss (l). **77 Alamy Images:** Stephen Vowles. **120 Garden World Images:** F. Davis. **125 Andrew Lawson. 129** www.wigglywigglers.co.uk. **136 Nicola Browne:** Designer: Isabelle Greene. **146 GAP Photos Ltd:** John Glover/Design: Land Art, Hampton Court Flower Show 2000. **149 DK Images:** Jacqui Hurst (bc). **156 Modeste Herwig. 158 GAP Photos Ltd:** John Glover (cr); Juliette Wade (bc). **Garden World Images:** (bl) & A. Graham (br); **The Garden Collection:** Torie Chugg (tc). **Garden Picture Library:** John Glover (cl). **Garden Exposures Photo Library:** Andrea Jones (tl). **Clive Nichols:** (c). **Courtesy of Thompson & Morgan** (tr). **164 Clive Nichols:** Vale End, Surrey. **184 John Tarren/David Scrivener Archive. 185 John Tarren/David Scrivener Archive** (tr) (c) & (br). **218 GAP Photos Ltd:** Paul Debois (bc) (br). **Garden Picture Library:** Howard Rice (bl). **The Garden Collection:** Derek St Romaine (cr). **226 Garden Picture Library. 227 Courtesy of Jotul As. 230** Cut flower statistics supplied by The *Ecologist.* **239 John Tarren/**

David Scrivener Archive. 241 Eye Ubiquitous: G Redmayne (tl). **259 Garden Picture Library:** Botanica (bl). **261 Marianne Majerus Photography:** Designer: Stephen Crisp. **277 Corbis:** O'Brien Productions. **281 Corbis:** Robert Dowling (br). **295 John Tarren/David Scrivener Archive. 306 Ardea:** Kenneth W. Fink (tl). **FLPA:** Foto Natura Stock (tr). **307 Corbis:** James Marshall (tl). **FLPA:** R P Lawrence (tc). **OSF:** Gary Griffen (tr). **314 Alamy Images:** Alex Hess (clb). **Cephas Picture Library:** Peter Barr (cla); John Davies (bl). **Modeste Herwig:** (bc). **Ken Muir Ltd:** (tl). **Fred Lyon:** (ca). **Courtesy of Flag Hill Winery & Distillery, Lee, New Hampshire, USA:** (crb). **Photos Horticultural:** (tr). **334 ArdeaLondon** (bl). **Courtesy of British Pig Executive** (fbr). **Corbis:** Robert Dowling (bc). **DK Images:** Weald and Downland Open Air Museum, Chichester (cl). **Ecoscene:** Frank Blackburn (tr). **FLPA:** Sarah Rowland (c)

DK would like to thank the following people for help with location photographs:
Daphne Lambert of Penrhos Court, Kington (food); Jane Howard (smallholding livestock and bees); Saskia Marjoram (cut flowers); Ticklemore Cheese, Totnes; James & Karen Skevington (ducks and geese).

Sheherazade Goldsmith would like to thank: Annie Gatti, Erica Bower, Daphne Lambert, Matilda Lee, Pat Thomas and Robert Yarham; everyone at DK who worked on the book; The *Ecologist*; Richard and Kirsty; and my husband, Zac.